Published by Clovercroft Publishing, Franklin, Tennessee

Edited by OnFire Books

Copy Edit by David Brown

Cover Design by Nelly Sanchez

Interior Design by Suzanne Lawing

Printed in the United States of America

978-1-950892-31-0

DEDICATION

I dedicate this book to my two children, Tori and Grayson, my grandson Cooper, all my unborn grandchildren (and I hope there are many), and the two people that taught me the most about doing the right thing as I grew up; my mother and father, Jane and the late Dewey Faught. May the following words forever provide a beacon of light to guide your steps as you travel down life's highway. I love and cherish you all.

ACKNOWLEDGMENTS

I'd like to acknowledge several talented people that were very instrumental in making my book come to be. Thank you Tammy Kling and the OnFire Books team whose expertise and guidance are the reasons my book made it to print. A special thanks to Tiarra Tompkins who walked every step of this two-year journey with me. Your love and support gave me the fortitude to see the light at the end of this tunnel. And lastly, a big I LOVE YOU to my wonderful daughter, Tori, who was the sounding board for dozens of ideas and revisions, and never once told her daddy, "that's bad writing." God Bless you all, and I thank you from the bottom of my heart!

CONTENTS

PROLOGUE

A DAY AT THE RACES

I was extremely excited, rushing to get my bet down for the last race, and not really paying close attention to anything else. This was the single largest horse racing winning ticket I had ever cashed, and my exhilaration was palpable. My anxiousness was making the cashier a little nervous herself, so when she said, "And after your bet, I owe you $2,463.50," the amount didn't really sink in. It was my bet of the day, and I knew I had won quite a bit, but I didn't realize it was that much. I collected the stack of one hundred dollar bills and merrily went off to find Mark (my racing buddy) to watch the last race. Horse racing is my one guilty pleasure, and all of this was taking place at Oaklawn Racing Casino Resort in Hot Springs, Arkansas, during the 2018 race meet.

I found Mark in our usual spot just as the last race started. The horses came charging down the stretch, the pounding of their hooves mingling with the thunderous cheers of encouragement and hope. Our horse didn't win, so we grabbed our stuff and headed to my truck for the one-hour ride home. That's when it hit me...something wasn't **RIGHT**. I was still amazed that I had won that much money, but now that feeling was starting to come over me. You all know the feeling I'm talking about. All of us have had it hundreds of times in our lives. It's that feeling way down in the pit of our stomach… that nagging tug on our conscience…that little voice telling us, you know better. And we do. We all know better. For the most part, we know when something isn't **RIGHT**.

It's whether or not we choose to listen to that still, small voice or ignore it. By this time, I had done the math several times in my head and I KNEW Joan (the cashier) had paid me too much money. But I couldn't figure out how she could have miscalculated. Everything in Oaklawn's wagering system is automated, so a mistake is very, very rare. "Forget about it," the other voice in my head kept saying. "You won the race and they paid you the money. Race closed."

"Oh no, this race isn't closed," shot back the voice of **RIGHT**.

About halfway home, I knew what I had to do. If they paid me too much money, I had to give it back. Mark and I had already planned on going back to the track the next day, so I made it a point to get there a little early to take care of this.

I'll never forget the look on Joan's face when she looked up and saw me walking toward her window. "It's YOU," she shrieked, somewhat in disbelief, a wave of obvious relief washing over her. "I can't believe you came back," she continued. "You know I made a mistake in your payout yesterday, **RIGHT**?"

"Yes ma'am, I don't know what you did, but I had a feeling it was too much."

"He came back!" she shouted to her two co-workers on each side, who were now observing our conversation. They looked like they had had an Elvis sighting. They were equally shocked that I came back. Joan had obviously shared our encounter from the day before when she realized her register was off.

Joan had keyed in the wrong amount of my wager for the last race and that threw all her numbers off for my payout. After much calculating and ciphering, as we like to say in Arkansas, she and her boss calculated that she had paid me $1,502.50 TOO MUCH. So, I calmly took the same large wad of one hundred dollar bills out of my pocket, counted out that exact amount, and handed it to her. She carefully re-counted it and put it in her register. The look on her face as she turned back to me was worth a thousand times more than that. With tears in her eyes, and pure gratitude in every word, she said, "I can't thank you enough for coming back. I would have had to pay all of that had you not returned. My register was still short about $1,000, but that was my fault in how I rang up your last bet. I have to pay that." I assured her that the pleasure was mine and apologized for any confusion I may have contributed to.

As I returned to my seat and shared with Mark what had happened, I heard it again. That stupid little voice…dang it! It was back. "What??? What else do you want me to do? I gave the money back…I did the **RIGHT** thing," I tried to convince myself. But it wouldn't stop. That voice wouldn't stop saying, "but what about the rest of the money?"

"That wasn't my fault. She entered the wrong amount, that was her fault," I tried to argue with myself. "But you were rushing her. She was caught up in YOUR excitement, and you were rushing her to get your last bet down."

"That's her job," came back the voice of reason in my little pea brain.

"You were partly responsible for causing her mistake. You

were rushing her," came the now familiar voice of **RIGHT** that I couldn't escape.

It wouldn't stop…"It's partly your fault too. Shared responsibility, isn't that what you always say, Brian Faught?" You know you're in trouble when the voice in your head goes third person on you.

By the fourth race, I couldn't take it anymore. I took the now much smaller wad of hundreds out of my pocket, peeled five of them off and headed to Joan's window. She beamed as she looked up and saw me coming. But she thought I was just going to place another bet. I walked up to the window, leaned in so it was just her and I in that moment in time, and said, "God laid it on my heart to do this," as I handed her the $500. "I was partly responsible for your mistake," I explained, "so I should be responsible for some of the cost of that mistake." She was both dumbfounded and grateful beyond words. She just stared at the money, then me, then the money again. "It's the **RIGHT** thing to do, Joan," I assured her, as we both enjoyed the moment.

I lost my butt on horse racing that day, but I won something that money can't buy…PEACE! The peace that comes when we listen to that still, small voice in our head and heart. The voice that always tells us what the **RIGHT** thing is, if we'll just listen. And that's what the rest of this book is about; how to learn to listen to that voice. The voice of **RIGHT** .

Doing the **RIGHT** thing cost me $2,002.50 that day. Or did it? How do you calculate what doing the wrong thing costs you? And how do you measure what doing the **RIGHT** thing might do for you going forward? I gave all that money back plus some, and completely did the **RIGHT** thing, so you'd think the **RIGHT** Gods would have smiled on me and I'd have a banner day at the track. Wrong, racing boy…I got hammered by the ponies that day. So why did I do it? Because I'm writing a book called, *The Power of Right*? Because I have a company called "Just Do the Right Thing?" Because I was raised to know better? And why did it take that voice's repeated naggings, I mean reminders, to get me to do the **RIGHT** thing? All of these questions will be answered in the following pages. But to sum it all up in a Reader's Digest version; I did all this because I'm human. Because right isn't always easy…and **RIGHT** isn't always cheap…and **RIGHT** isn't always black and white. It's our human tendency to be drawn to the path of least resistance, and a lot of times that path doesn't exactly line up with the path of **RIGHT**. The following pages will give you a very clear understanding of how to use **RIGHT** to get the things you want and love the most in life.

WHAT IS RIGHT?

Everyone has a general idea of the concept of **RIGHT**. In every country and every culture, there is a universal code of what is **RIGHT** and wrong that governs people. The one thing that makes this book different from any other you will read is that you may know what **RIGHT** is, but I am going to teach you how to not only understand what **RIGHT** truly is, but how to get **RIGHT** inside of you, and how to make **RIGHT** part of your identity. When that happens, every time you are faced with a moral dilemma, or a decision at work, or a conflict with a co-worker, or an issue with your spouse, there is no question that you will always choose to do the **RIGHT** thing every time.

Why is this important? The question has to be asked. What will doing the **RIGHT** thing do for you in your personal life? How will it affect your relationships? What will it mean for your professional career? Continue reading and see how **RIGHT** will change every aspect of your life.

The power of right is a technique that combines doing the **RIGHT** thing with the power of a question. In the following chapters, we will very clearly lay out what **RIGHT** in our society represents, but it's important to understand how to get to **RIGHT**. You have a far greater chance of finishing something

"Starting at RIGHT is never wrong"

the **RIGHT** way if you consistently learn how to **start at right,** to start it the **RIGHT** way. Everyone has a baseline understanding of **RIGHT**. If you start your decisions, your conversations, your meetings, your calls, or whatever it is you're about to start doing, and if you will start at the point that you know to be **RIGHT**, you will greatly increase your chances of finishing that endeavor the **RIGHT** way as well. **"Starting at RIGHT"** is going to involve a one-word question queue that will trigger your commitment to starting everything you do the same way, the **RIGHT** way, every time. That one-word question queue is, Just? And the answer, as you will come to know very clearly is, "Do the **RIGHT** thing." Just, in this situation, means only. So, Just? do the **RIGHT** thing in essence means, "The only thing you have to do is what is **RIGHT**." And you will now apply that principle to everything you do in your life. Every single situation in your life will now start with the very simple trigger, Just? And I'm sure you will agree that if you learn to do the **RIGHT** thing, make the **RIGHT** decision, say the **RIGHT** thing, and associate with the **RIGHT** people, then if everything you do is **RIGHT** your life HAS TO GET BETTER!

WHAT IS A TRIGGER AND WHAT DOES IT MEAN?

If you truly want to get **RIGHT** inside of you, you have to understand what a trigger is, and why it's so effective as a behavior management tool in your life. *Triggering events happen when we respond out of habit, or out of a knee jerk* reaction to unexpected circumstances or moments. This happens to us all.

The trigger itself can be just about anything—a colleague says something offensive; a participant in a meeting makes snarky comments; you read an inflammatory post on social media; or a family member pushes your buttons at a gathering when you're already stressed. A trigger can also be from something positive. How many people reading this right now absolutely light up when your grandchild walks into the room? How many of you instantly feel better, even excited when you look down at your caller ID and see it's your spouse or your best friend calling to check on you?

All too often, we react unconsciously on automatic pilot, and do or say things we later regret.

"Just? now becomes the one-word trigger that will change your life forever"

Instead, we can learn the tools to *identify* and *interrupt* the cycle of events that happen when we're triggered. Keep reading for more ideas and tools!

THE VOICE

Understanding the power of a trigger, one word, JUST, posed as a question, now becomes the most important word in your life…because it affects EVERYTHING. Every aspect of your life is now triggered by that one word. The key is that it's triggered for the **RIGHT** response. It will trigger you to respond intelligibly, a decision, instead of react instinctively, a condition. By using the trigger to activate your cognition, we will forever change the way we interact with people and the

"A Question hijacks your brain and makes you stop and think."

circumstances surrounding our lives. One word now becomes the VOICE you listen to. The quality of your life, good or bad, is dictated by the voice in your head. What you think about (which is just the voice in your head), you will speak about. What you speak about, you will bring about. The rest of this book is meant to give you the tools you need to change the way you talk to yourself.

THE POWER OF A QUESTION

The power of a question is an integral part of this book and *The Power of Right*. Science has long acknowledged the power of a question. Questions will hijack your brain. The moment you hear one, you literally can't think of anything else. That is a powerful tool. A question, by its very nature, makes you stop and think. When you stop and think for a split second, you have a better chance of making the **RIGHT** decision. It really is that simple. Far too often, we react to a situation, instead of taking a moment to think and respond. How many times have we all said, "What was I thinking? Why did I do that?" It's very clear that we weren't thinking or responding intelligibly. We were reacting instinctively, which is something everyone does many times a day. By training yourself to use that one-word question, Just? as a prelude to every thought, every action, and every sentence, you are training yourself to THINK BEFORE YOU SPEAK OR ACT. And here's how it works. Just? now acts as a pattern interrupt mechanism in your thought process. The trigger, Just? interrupts the unwanted behavior or thought pattern, and the answer, do the **RIGHT** thing, suggests a more suitable behavior or thought pattern. And because you make the suggestion yourself, you're far more likely to act out on the new direction you're giving yourself. People don't argue with their own conclusions. Even when it's YOU, TALKING TO YOU. When you self-direct, you're far more likely to actually see that thought or action through.

WHAT HAPPENS IN THE BRAIN?

When we're asked a question, our whole brain is instantly on duty. The happy hormone serotonin is released and that causes your brain to go into thinking gear and makes it easier to find answers and develop solutions. This mental reflex is known as instinctive elaboration. When our brain thinks about the answer to a question, it literally can't think about anything else!

If you're the person asking the question, then that power goes to you. Your question is the only thing that that person can think about. Think about the concept of multitasking. Even if you think you're someone who can multitask, think again. Research has shown that humans are not good at multitasking or equipped to multitask. Even if we think we're someone who is.

It is asking people the **RIGHT** questions, instead of telling them what to do, that gives them the greatest chance for success. Questions push people to figure out the answers on their own. Instead of giving the answer, a question gives that person (you) an opportunity to learn. The question system has been used by corporate executives, successful salespeople, coaches of elite athletes, and almost all therapists. It's instrumental in helping people discover their specific way of thinking and whatever mental blocks or blind spots that person may have. It gives them a way to change their mindset while creating and achieving their goals. You can't change your life without first changing your mindset. You can't change your mindset without changing the way you talk to yourself. You can't change the way you talk to yourself until you start accessing new information and using that to change the narrative in your mind. The best way to access new information is to ask questions.

The method is quite simple. Asking the **RIGHT** questions gives people the answers they need to move forward in life. Let's use our dreams as an example. Many people stop following their dreams when they grow up, choosing instead to find something to support themselves until retirement. Instead we need to look at our dreams practically. They aren't something that is out of reach. They are the wants and desires of our heart that we have to figure out HOW to reach. Dreams are called dreams for a reason—they are something better than what we have now. To achieve what's better, we have to start finding new solutions; we have to learn new ways to think.

Dan Lange, the very successful track and field coach for the University of Southern California, trains based on the use of questions. Every day, he asks everybody how they feel. Answering fine was not a suitable answer. You had to be precise with the answer to this question to understand how you felt physically, mentally, and emotionally. Depending on the answers you provided, Dan would lay out the training for the day with the intention of pushing you to get the best results. With this method, Lange's athletes learned how much their mental and emotional states affected results and how to improve. They were building themselves from the core out.

Here are the benefits of asking questions. You can start asking today.

YOUR WHOLE LIFE HAS BEEN SHAPED BY THE QUESTIONS YOU'VE ASKED

There are more scientific articles than I could cite here to prove that we learn about life by asking questions. Think about children. They naturally start learning about the world by watching, and many times by asking the question most parents get tired of hearing. "Why?" This is how kids learn the results of questions and the meanings of words. It shows them how to interact in their own relationships as they grow.

– IF WE ASK MORE QUESTIONS, WE WILL GET MORE AND EVEN BETTER ANSWERS

As we get older, and with age and responsibilities, the questioning begins to lessen, and we settle for the answers that we have learned to this point. The minute what we know doesn't apply, we get stuck. Whenever we experience a problem or roadblock, our brain begins to run a diagnostic on all of our life experiences similar to the current situation. It is looking for a pattern or an answer that it recognizes. This is why we sometimes have illogical reactions: If we do not give time for the brain to find a better solution, it is going to revert to established patterns and go with what it knows. Asking questions gives us a chance to learn more. And the more information and experiences we have, the larger our database of options will be when we have to solve a problem.

– HOW YOU LIVE AND HOW WELL YOU LIVE WILL BE BALANCED BY THE QUESTIONS YOU ARE WILLING TO ASK

> "The quality of your thinking is determined by the quality of your questions, for questions are the engine, the driving force of thinking"

It may sound cliché, but your life and how well you live is influenced directly by what you think. "The quality of our thinking, in turn, is determined by the quality of our questions, for questions are the engine, the driving force behind thinking."—*The Miniature Guide to the Art of Asking Essential Questions*

– BEING ABLE TO ASK QUESTIONS MEANS YOU ARE OPEN TO NEW ANSWERS

Learning and questioning will help grow new neural pathways and create new patterns in your brain. The more pathways and patterns, the more flexible it is. With increased flexibility, you will be able to access the information you have stored in your brain, instead of responding with old responses (patterns) that you are used to.

– ASKING QUESTIONS INCREASES YOUR WISDOM

Wisdom comes from being more open, which is having more flexibility in your brain. This changes the way you see things (your perception) and when you start to make important decisions, your biases will decrease! Being open to the world around you and the differing perceptions of others will greatly increase your likelihood of finding lasting happiness.

– WHEN YOU ASK THE RIGHT QUESTIONS, YOU WILL CREATE MORE JOY

We all have an idea of what peace and harmony in our lives should look and feel like. Most of us have never sat down and discovered what causes these feelings. When we ask ourselves the deep question, what can I do to feel more joy and more peace, we can start to understand how to feel at peace more often. It starts with the realization that we are the creators of our feelings; they don't just happen to us.

Your inner work begins by asking yourself simple but deep questions:

What makes me happy in life?

How do I manage the problems in my life and still make myself happy?

> "We are the creators of our feelings; they don't just happen to us."

What do I do every day to move myself toward my goals in life?

Then start asking yourself more difficult questions:

What is the most important thing in my life? How do I support that which is so important?

What else can I do to make this area of my life better?

The more times we ask ourselves important questions, the easier it gets to accept ourselves and to take charge in changing our lives for the better.

DECISIONS OR CONDITIONS

These are the two ways your life is controlled. Your thoughts direct one of them, decisions, and your emotions feed the other, conditions. In that moment you receive a trigger, your thoughts or your emotions are going to take over and determine what happens next. Either you're going to use your mind to make a decision and control the moment, or your emotions are going to take the lead, prompting a knee jerk reaction and allowing the moment (your conditions) to control you. The purpose of this program is to give you a tool to make your thoughts stronger than your emotions. When that is the case, you get to choose which one of these two, decisions or conditions, controls your life.

"Make your thoughts stronger than your emotions"

By making you stop and think for a split second, the power of a question is forcing you to make a decision. Every time you have the luxury of thinking about your response, you have a greater chance of making the **RIGHT** choice. That is a decision. The lack of this thought process leaves you reacting to whatever situation you are faced with. In this case, the situation, the condition, is what is dictating what you do next, so it is controlling your life at that moment. Here are a few relevant examples:

– You have spent weeks planning a beach picnic trip with your family. The kids are excited and everyone is ready to go. You wake up in the morning to the sounds of storms and you see lightning flashing in your window. You can tell that everyone is disappointed and this is the pivotal moment when you have a choice. This condition can ruin the day or you could change your plans. Luckily, you would never let rain ruin a perfectly good family day. With quick thinking, you say "OK gang, plan B; we are going out for our favorite sushi lunch, then to the theater to see that movie we've all been talking about."

Your decision to save the family outing has made the conditions irrelevant.

– You have been planning National Sales Meeting Saturday for your company for three years, and you personally are proud of the agenda you've put together. Your past events have led the four hundred plus participants to expect a lot and you have lined up an incredible keynote speaker to be part of the event. You had tried to hire him the previous two years, but the schedules just didn't work. During your final walk-through, you receive a call from his assistant and your chosen keynote speaker has the flu and will not be making the trip…a condition. You could panic. Instead, you take a deep breath and quickly go into plan B mode and start reviewing your options…a decision. You know you have two or three very qualified speakers in your sales group that would love the honor of speaking to the whole organization. But with very little time to prepare, a quality presentation was a long shot. Understanding that, you decide to use them all. Breaking down the time slot into three relevant talks by qualified people that love the company saves the day!

Both of these examples show the potential for the condition to ruin your day, and how having the willingness to think past the condition to make an appropriate decision puts you in a position to make the most of the occasion, no matter what it is. We are all faced with these moments every day. By programming yourself to always count on your decisions to rule the day, you prevent unwanted conditions from dictating the quality of your life. Your thoughts are stronger than your emotions!

The biggest point here is that you can only control you.

Ask yourself, "Am I focused on the things I can control or the things I can't control in my life?" Most of us have heard the Serenity Prayer. It applies so much to each and every one of our lives. "God, grant me the serenity to accept the things I cannot change,/ The courage to change the things I can,/ And the wisdom to know the difference."

So often we find ourselves focused on what we can't control and it can cause a great deal of stress. Think about any moment in life where someone hurt you. How did you respond? In every situation, you can't control how someone else treats you, but you can control how you respond.

Once you decide to focus on something (regardless if it is the **RIGHT** thing to focus on or not), your mind instinctively shifts to the next decision. You then start learning how to connect a series of good decisions, successful decisions, to get the things you want. Success in life is nothing more than a series of successful decisions.

Are you ready for change?

MINDFULNESS

The next thing a question does is bring you into a state of mindfulness. There is abundant research that suggests the practice of mindfulness is a very big factor in extended or long-term happiness. Why? When you are focused solely on the present, you're not worrying or stressing about problems you may have stemming from your past, and you're not longing or wishing for anything in the future. You're making the most and getting the most out of the moment you're in. And that's the whole concept behind *The Power of Right*. By using the one-word question queue, Just? to trigger your thought process, you're making yourself come back to the moment and address the issue at hand. It doesn't get any easier than that. Life is about the moment, and success in life is nothing more than a series of successful moments.

"MINDFULNESS – a mental state achieved by focusing one's awareness on the present moment"

By definition, mindfulness is: "A mental state achieved by focusing one's awareness on the present moment, while calmly acknowledging and accepting one's feelings, thoughts, and bodily sensations; often used as a therapeutic technique." A question, by its very nature, makes you stop and think about what has been asked of you in that moment. So, a question brings you into a state of mindfulness by making you focus on the moment you are in and nothing else. So, instead of a knee jerk reaction, you can actually pause and make a choice with thought, not emotion. It will benefit you every time. Your thoughts have to be stronger than your emotions.

If you do some research on mindfulness at mindful.org, they have laid out exactly what it means to be mindful.

"Mindfulness is the basic human ability to be fully present, aware of where we are and what we're doing, and not overly reactive or overwhelmed by what's going on around us."

Eight Things to Know About Mindfulness:

1. **Mindfulness is not obscure or exotic.** It's familiar to us because it's what we already do, how we already are. It takes many shapes and goes by many names.

2. **Mindfulness is not a special added thing we do.** We

already have the capacity to be present, and it doesn't require us to change who we are. But we can cultivate these innate qualities with simple practices that are scientifically demonstrated to benefit ourselves, our loved ones, our friends and neighbors, the people we work with, and the institutions and organizations we take part in.

3. **You don't need to change.** Solutions that ask us to change who we are or become something we're not have failed us over and over again. Mindfulness recognizes and cultivates the best of who we are as human beings.

4. **Mindfulness has the potential to become a transformative social phenomenon.** Here's why:

5. **Anyone can do it.** Mindfulness cultivates universal human qualities and does not require anyone to change their beliefs. Everyone can benefit and it's easy to learn.

6. **It's a way of living.** Mindfulness is more than just a practice. It brings awareness and caring into everything we do—and it cuts down on needless stress. Even a little makes our lives better.

7. **It's evidence-based.** We don't have to take mindfulness by faith. Both science and experience demonstrate its positive benefits for our health, happiness, work, and relationships.

8. **It sparks innovation.** As we deal with our world's increasing complexity and uncertainty, mindfulness can lead us to effective, resilient, and low-cost responses to seemingly insurmountable problems.

THE POWER OF RIGHT

The Power of Right is the conscious effort to put **RIGHT** to work in your life. It's a technique that combines doing the **RIGHT** thing with the power of a question, with the goal of helping you **start at right** in all your decision making. You have a much better chance of finishing something the **RIGHT** way if you learn to consistently start the **RIGHT** way. When you start thinking about **RIGHT**, or witnessing **RIGHT** behavior, **RIGHT** gets "on you."

When **RIGHT** gets ON YOU, it creates a behavior. When this happens, you start looking for ways to do **RIGHT** by people. You slow down in traffic to let cars in, you volunteer at church or the local hospital, or you offer to babysit for free for your single mother neighbor. You look for ways to do the **RIGHT** thing. After a while, you will wake up one day and realize that now **RIGHT** is "in you".

When **RIGHT** gets IN YOU, it becomes part of your identity. When that happens, your life is changed forever. That is when three major life transformations happen. First, you begin to reap the reward of **RIGHT** in your life. When you are **RIGHT** -centered, you begin to harvest the spoils of two of the strongest laws of human nature: the law of attraction and the law of reciprocity. The Law of Attraction basically means that what you put out into the world is what you will attract back. If you are kind and decent and respectful to people, that is the kind of behavior you will attract back to you. If you put positive energy into the people and places you encounter, you will receive positive energy back. What you put out is what you get back. The Law of Reciprocity is similar. It means that people will treat you like you treat them. If you are sensitive and empathetic to your friends and family, they will show you those same genuine characteristics.

Secondly, when people see you always doing the **RIGHT** thing and always starting at **RIGHT** in your decision making, they begin to factor that into the decisions they make regarding you. The best indicator of future behavior is past, relevant behavior. When people see you repeatedly acting in a certain manner, doing the **RIGHT** thing over and over and over, and making the **RIGHT** decisions in both your professional and personal life, they rightfully assume that you will continue acting that way in the future. Consider this, you are among three employees up for a promotion at your place of work. All three of you have the same educational background, the same basic work skill sets, and the same level of experience. But you are the one that has the "**RIGHT** factor" working in your favor. You're always on time, you always treat everyone with respect, and you can always be counted on to do whatever it takes to get the job done. Your boss has come to expect this of you and that becomes the differentiator in the decision for the promotion; you get the call every time. The same applies to your personal life. Friends, family, and your extended circle of influence all know that you have a **RIGHT** minded approach to everything in your life. You do the **RIGHT** thing, period. That's just what you do. That's who you are. When people know and expect that, their attitude about you reflects that. They want to associate with you. They want you around. People are attracted to **RIGHT** because they've seen the positive side effects that

> "The best indicator of future behavior is past, relevant behavior."

typically accompany **RIGHT** minded people and situations.

And lastly, YOU WIN!!! You win the battle in your mind. Every day, we're all faced with dozens of decisions to make, and oftentimes, these decisions can get a little complicated. Doing the **RIGHT** thing isn't always the easy thing or the popular thing or the convenient thing to do. So, we struggle in our minds with what is the appropriate decision. This struggle repeats itself many times a day, creating anxiety, stress, anxiousness, indecision, and a host of other feelings. Well, when **RIGHT** gets in you and becomes your identity, those struggles are over. You know that you **start at right** for all your decisions, so that question is settled. And starting at **RIGHT** sets the tone for you to follow WHAT YOU KNOW TO BE RIGHT throughout that decision process, so there's no conflict in your mind. You know what you're going to do. You know where you're going to start, and doing that, you have a better idea of where you're going to finish. Anxiety about what to do, how to start…eliminated. You've just made sure that your thoughts are stronger than your emotions.

HOW WILL THEY REMEMBER YOU?

In business, if they don't remember you, YOU'RE DONE! When they (your customers) don't remember you…YOU don't get a chance to bid on the big project, they don't accept your calls, and you're not invited to the yearly golf tournament. You're not….you fill in the blanks because it's your career that's being damaged. In short, if they don't remember you in business, you're out! You're

> "People remember how you make the feel."

done! In your personal life, if they don't remember you, you just miss a bunch of cool stuff. You miss the birthday party which you weren't invited to. You miss watching the football game with the group because they just didn't think to call you. You miss the intimate luncheon with the girls because they couldn't remember if you liked small gatherings. In all these cases, you just didn't leave enough of an impression on people for them to remember to include you in things or events that you would possibly enjoy and fit into. HOW WILL PEOPLE REMEMBER YOU? There are many ways for you to leave a lasting impression on people in both a professional and personal setting. Don't forget that people remember how they feel about most situations. When they don't remember partic-ular conversations or things that happened, they will remember the emotional impact, or lack thereof, those situations had on them. So, you making the extra effort to con-

> "When people leave your presence, what are they saying to themselves about you?"

nect with people about things that interest THEM will leave them with fond thoughts about you and the exchange you had with them (find out what they love and give it to them). Think about that for a moment. When people leave your presence, what are they saying to themselves about you?

"He is always so considerate."

"She is always dressed to a T."

"She makes me feel good every time I'm around her."

"He is the most polite person I've ever met."

"He's just so nice."

Are these the types of things that people say about you? Or is it something like this...

"What a jerk!"

"Who does she think she is?"

"That guy was looking right through me. How rude!"

"How arrogant can a guy be?"

People are saying something about us, and we get to choose what, for the most part. So, how can you positively impact people so they leave your presence feeling much the better for having been in it? People remember how you make them feel, so taking the focus off you and putting it on them is a great place to start. But having great relationships isn't just about making people feel good. There's got to be some substance also. People have a real need to feel valued and significant to the people around them. So taking a genuine interest in people AND THE THINGS THAT ARE IMPORTANT TO THEM is the perfect way to show them you care.

So what are some character traits that people notice and appreciate?

–Positive attitude   –Trustworthy   –Enthusiastic
–Respectful   –Integrity   –Friendly
–Honorable   –High energy   –Outgoing
–Charismatic   –Personable   –Kind
–Professional   –Classy   –Thoughtful
–Knowledgeable   –Organized   –Helpful
–Credible   –Detailed
–Disciplined   –Polite

You get the point, right? Simple things that EVERYONE appreciates receiving from other people are the things that get you remembered for the **RIGHT** reasons. Study your interactions with others to see if you are making the kind of impression you want. There are many ways to be memorable and you should focus on a few that are in your core wheelhouse. This is an exercise that can have a huge payoff in both your professional and personal life. Being remembered is the first step to being included, appreciated, and I hate to say, liked. Face it, it's way easier going through life when the majority of people that you interact with LIKE YOU!

In business, being remembered is imperative. Failing to do so can literally cost you your job or your business, because the consequences of being forgotten are potentially catastrophic: no bid, no promotion, and exclusion …all the beginning of the end. In most situations in life, not being remembered is not an enviable position to be in.

> "Always doing the RIGHT thing is enough to get people to remember you."

So, will doing the **RIGHT** thing get you remembered by the people in your life? Will your client remember that you willingly pointed out a billing mistake on their behalf? Will your teammate recall that you volunteered to take the extra shift so she, a single mother, could spend the holiday with her kids? Will your friend acknowledge that you dropping them off and picking them up from the airport, thus saving them those exorbitant airport parking fees, is the mark of a true friend? You can name dozens of other examples that all point to you doing **RIGHT** by someone in your life, and it making a lasting impression on them. Always doing the **RIGHT** thing, and all that that entails, is ENOUGH, in the vast majority of instances, to have people REMEMBER YOU!

ENERGY – LIFE'S GREAT MAGNET

We're drawn to it, like a moth to an open flame...we all recognize it, even when we're not sure if it's good or bad... we all have it, whether we know what to do with it or not. It's ENERGY, and you really need to harness what you've got and learn how to use it. People are attracted to energy. We all know those people...it's not just what they say, it's how they say it; the conviction, the enthusiasm, the belief, the charisma. It's not just how they dress, it's how they carry the clothes they've chosen; body symmetry, flowing, strength, confidence...style. It's not just how they make you feel, it's the intensity of the feelings you have every time you're in their presence; excited, challenged, fulfilled, significant...FULL OF LIFE. People love energy because we all have it and we recognize its effect on everyone around us. Energy, like all other behavior character-istics, is contagious. So, what are you spreading?

There are many different ways your energy manifests itself into your life...your thoughts, your expressions, your body language, your tone, your ATTITUDE (emphasis provided because this is the most important), your pace, your vocabu-lary, your intellect, your posture, your desire, your conviction, your dreams...energy has many forms and we are all good at displaying a couple of them. Harness that...understand that... use that...capitalize on that...refine that! It doesn't matter how your body and personality choose to release their energy. What matters is that you recognize your delivery mechanism, and whether or not it attracts others to you or pushes them away. Is it positive or negative energy that you're known for? Is the glass half full, or did you break the glass? Do people look up and smile when they see you coming? Or do you catch the glimpsing turn as people avoid your look and thus any exchange with you? Many of us can't help, nor can we change, how we put off energy. It's just who we are and what we do. What we can change, however, is the intensity and quality of the vibes we're giving the rest of the world. Everyone can get excited about something. Everyone can be uplifting to someone. We all have the capacity to be passionate and to share that passion with others. The point here is that energy is power, and power is **RIGHT**. People will REMEMBER you by your energy or the lack thereof. They will remember how you ignited the rest of the group with your out of the box thinking and suggestions. They will remember the soft side of you that took the time to call after their mother's surgery. They will be drawn to your unwavering principles of **RIGHT** and good and all that they stand for. People are attracted to energy. What kind are you putting out? Is it your calling card, or your Achilles heel?

WRITE IT DOWN

Dear Reader,

This book is more than just a list of lessons that will change your life. Any book can do that. This book is an interactive way to get **RIGHT** into your life. At the end of every lesson, you will find a list of questions and an exercise. These questions and exercises will change this book from enlightening reading to changing your life forever. You know about *the power of right* and the power of a question, and now you're going to become intimately aware of the power of writing it down. These questions will cover the material on that particular principle and WHAT YOU PLAN ON DOING WITH IT. If you can, answer these questions before you move on to the next principle, while the information is still fresh on your mind. Each principle is a building block to the next. Recent studies show that writing a goal down increases the likelihood of accomplishing that goal by 42 percent. That's a staggering

> "Recent studies show you are 42 percent more likely to reach a goal if you write it down"

statistic and makes the exercise well worth the effort.

Writing things down affects you on two different levels: it gets it in your head (encoding) and it gets it on paper. A notebook, a diary, a folder in your computer; you get the idea. If the information is somewhere easily accessible, and you forget it, you can easily retrieve it and use it.

But there's another phenomenon occurring when you write things down called encoding. Encoding is the process that our brain undergoes as it receives and analyzes information. In this process, the mind determines what information to keep in our long-term memory, and what information to disregard. Writing things down greatly enhances the encoding process and makes it much more likely that the information will be remembered.

Writing things down also triggers what's called the generation effect, which simply states that an individual is far more likely to remember something that they have generated themselves. When you write your goals down, or write the answers to important questions, you actually use this effect twice; once when you think of the goal, and a second time when you write it down. With all this cognitive processing going on, you are literally searing the goal into your brain.

And lastly, writing goals and answers down utilizes both

> "Writing things down also triggers what's called the generation effect, which simply states that an individual is far more likely to remember something that they have generated themselves."

hemispheres of the brain. When you think of the goal, you are primarily using the **RIGHT** side, or imaginative part of your mind. But when you write those goals down, you are using the left hemisphere, or analytical part of your mind. The significance is that if you're only thinking about your goals or the information you read in these chapters, you are far less likely to implement the ideas or pursue the goals. But if you take the extra time and step of writing your thoughts and goals down at the end of each chapter, you are screaming to every fiber of your being that "you are serious, and you are going to accomplish these goals." Nuff said!

MEET ME IN THE MIRROR

Several years ago, I was contacted by the Arkansas Parole Officers Association about doing a presentation at their yearly conference. Several hundred parole officers and support staff gather to discuss their current issues and how to handle their business for the upcoming year. I gladly accepted and began putting the presentation together. In addition to the speech, I wanted something that each person, officers and parolees alike, could use every day, and have it serve as a queue every time they saw it to remind them to use the program. Because of the varying conditions this diverse group found themselves in (the parolees, that is), it was challenging to come up with the RIGHT piece. I kept trying to think of something that each person had in common, and it struck me that every morning all of them look in the mirror as they're getting ready for their day. So, I designed a mirror cling that listed the ten questions/answers of *the Power of Right*, with instructions to put it on the lower left-hand corner of their bathroom vanity mirror. Then, each morning, as you start your day, look down and ask the questions to YOURSELF and answer out loud. Looking at the mirror cling, ask out loud, "Just?" Then, look up at the "man in the mirror" and answer, "Do the **RIGHT** thing," out loud. Repeat the process for all ten questions/answers. In doing this, you're accomplishing several things:

– Asking the questions every day creates new neural pathways in your brain so when "life happens," your mind is already familiar with the ten principles and can easily apply one of them so you can correctly handle that situation. The context of the principles becomes second nature to you. Whatever repeatedly enters the mind, ultimately manifests itself into our actions.

– Speaking the questions/answers out loud holds you more accountable to that which you are speaking about. It's called "public declaration" and it's a powerful self-regulating tool.

– People don't argue with their own conclusions; when you say it, you own it. When you say it out loud every day, you completely start to own the behavior. It's something you accept as true and **RIGHT** ... something you believe...so you just do it.

"There's only two people you can't lie to; God and the man in the mirror."

Then, it struck me that not only was the mirror cling good for this particular group of people, it's the perfect prompt for EVERYONE. There are very few things that we all do every single morning, and looking into our vanity mirror is one of them. And I've been talking about this particular activity in my presentations for many years. I'm a strong believer that you have to talk to the "man in the mirror," or "the woman in the mirror."

This whole book is about the way you talk to yourself via the voice in your head, but it also involves speaking it into the universe. Speaking positive affirmations to yourself, ABOUT YOURSELF, out loud. You will hear me say throughout this book, "What you think about, you will speak about. What you speak about, you will bring about." There's only two people you can't lie to: God and the man in the mirror (that's you). As you come to realize this and accept this truth, your conversations with yourself become, or should become brutally honest. That's the purpose of the exercise. Once you acknowledge a situation, you are then able to correctly address it. As Dr. Phil so accurately states, "You can't change what you do not acknowledge."

When you speak it out loud, while you're looking yourself square in the eye, you know there's no place to hide. You know the truth. You know what you're capable of. You also know what your shortcomings are. There's no escaping the reality of your world. The time you spend each morning with the "man in the mirror" can be some of the most powerful self-awareness time you'll ever have, IF you're honest with yourself. The worst lies are the ones you tell yourself. Take this opportunity every morning to start your day the **RIGHT** way. Speak YOUR

> "What you think about, you will speak about. What you speak about, you will bring about."

TRUTH...the truth as it exists in your life today (you cannot change what you do not acknowledge). Call it like it is, as hard as that may be to do. When you acknowledge it, when you hear your own voice call out the good and the bad, you begin to accept it and thus can start changing it. You become your own biggest cheerleader. And that's as it should be because you're the only person that you can unequivocally count on. Parents, siblings, friends, co-workers, you name them... all people can potentially let you down and not be there for you when you need them. The voice in your head is the only voice you can 100 percent count on being there 100 percent of the time. Teach that voice to say the **RIGHT** things and your life will change forever. So, the phrase "MEET ME IN THE MIRROR" now becomes your queue to go look at "the man in the mirror" and get your mind **RIGHT**. Tell yourself the things that drive you, inspire you, motivate you, and that make you LOVE YOU!!!

You will also use the phrase to deal with other people and situations in your life. You might be in an argument with your spouse and you need to "meet me in the mirror" to figure out what your responsibility is and what is the **RIGHT** way to resolve the issue. You might "meet me in the mirror" to practice what you're going to say to your boss about the long overdue raise he promised you. You can "meet me in the mirror" to practice your sales pitch on the new products your company is offering. You can "meet me in the mirror" to talk about anything...that's what it's for...an opportunity for YOU to talk to YOU about anything that's important. And remember that, at times, your advice to yourself is to change the way you talk to yourself. You are what you repeatedly tell yourself you are. And sometimes that narrative needs a slight tune-up.

And remember, the mirror is just like life…just like *The Power of Right*: what you put into the mirror is exactly what you get back. What you put into life is exactly what you get back. When you put **RIGHT** out, you get **RIGHT** back. The mirror never lies…neither does life. When the smoke clears, and you're standing, looking at "the man in the mirror," know that you can build whatever kind of person you want.

"MEET ME IN THE MIRROR and let's start changing our lives."

The most important thing for you to take from "Meet Me in the Mirror" is an incredible degree of "self-love." Once you start that, get that, do that…you're on your way to experiencing the life you want. So, "MEET ME IN THE MIRROR" and let's start changing our lives.

Are you ready to get **RIGHT** into your life?

PRINCIPLE 1
JUST? DO THE RIGHT THING

There is a pivotal moment of truth in all of our lives when we realize that doing the **RIGHT** thing is the best way forward. Not everyone is lucky enough to have been raised to believe that and have to discover this lesson as they make their way through life. This moment of truth generally occurs when a heightened sense of emotion meets a heightened sense of awareness in a perfect storm of clarity. People remember what they feel. They may not remember exactly what was said or done, but they will always remember their emotional response to those words or actions. This is how people get addicted to doing **RIGHT**, feeling **RIGHT**, and putting forth **RIGHT** in all they do.

As humans, we like to replicate the things that make us feel good. When you do something **RIGHT**, like helping a sick neighbor with some yardwork, buying groceries for a single mother, or volunteering for the Feed the Seniors event at your church, you share in those feelings that make you feel good, the joy that **RIGHT** brings to other people. There is also a very real physical reaction to this joy, a chemical reward produced by your brain and deposited into your bloodstream called dopamine, also known as the feel-good chemical. Think about that for a moment. We are biologically hardwired to be rewarded for doing **RIGHT**. These are moments of truth. When you realize that **RIGHT** makes you feel good. When you realize that the rest of the world responds positively to **RIGHT**. When you witness firsthand the phenomenon of put **RIGHT** out, get **RIGHT** back. That's when it's easy to get **RIGHT** centered in your life.

> "We are biologically hardwired to be rewarded for doing RIGHT"

In every situation in life, there is a moment of truth, an emotional time during the exchange that people are likely to remember, and their recollections of the encounter can be very influential in their dealing with you and in how they choose to treat others as well. When something resonates with you, it will stay with you; when an applicable moment comes up, you will be able to fall back on that lesson and apply your experience, your truth. Choose to touch the lives of others with your moments of truth.

If doing the **RIGHT** thing, starting at **RIGHT**, really is the best way to go through life, let's talk about what **RIGHT** really means. First, starting at **RIGHT** is never wrong—**RIGHT** is RIGHT and wrong is wrong. It really is that black and white…most of the time. Over hundreds of years of recorded history, our cultures and societies in general have set a standard of **RIGHT**, a code of **RIGHT** if you will, that the people have agreed to follow. Over those years, the standard of **RIGHT** may have varied slightly or greatly as societal norms have progressed. But in all cases, society as a whole has agreed upon the new standard of **RIGHT**. Minds change, laws are altered, moral values shift, and people may accept new parameters for **RIGHT**. In the world we live in today, **RIGHT** as defined and accepted by society, is fairly well established.

Now, all that being said, there is a time that **RIGHT** actually does try to get away from black and white, and flirt with shades of gray. This is especially true when it comes to leadership, parenting, coaching, mentoring, and other influential positions in life. The gray, the blurred lines, come when **RIGHT** fights with easy. When **RIGHT** isn't popular, things can get a little uncomfortable. When **RIGHT** means losing money on a big business deal, everyone at the table has that fleeting thought of deviating from **RIGHT** just this one time. And the usual culprit that sets loose the gray animal in all of us is one of the most powerful forces in all of humanity, OUR EMOTIONS.

> "If you want to know what the RIGHT thing to do is, ask your mother"

In all my seminars and trainings, I advise people to always have a trusted advisor. Have someone in your professional and personal life that you can call, day or night, to get words of wisdom from. Or actually, what you're looking for are words of wisdom that are void of emotion. When you remove your own emotions from the equation (and **start at right**)), the picture becomes quite clear. If you want to know what the **RIGHT** thing to do is, ask your mother. She'll set you straight. I'm serious. Your mother is a great example of the aforementioned trusted advisor that will tell you the truth based on **RIGHT** as she knows it. And you'll listen to her…or you know what happens next. The saying "Mother knows best" has to come from somewhere, doesn't it?

Everyone has a previous frame of reference to almost everything that happens in their lives. And most often, **RIGHT** as we know it is black and white. But sometimes people have a different frame of reference, which may change how they perceive **RIGHT**. With different frames of reference, you may find that some people don't think of **RIGHT** the same way you do. Why is this? The answer, emotions. People emotionally process all of their life experiences differently. The way you frame **RIGHT**, for the most part (there are always exceptions), is a frame of reference that is universally accepted as different than wrong. There is a certain code of conduct that has been applied to our society and most people understand that framework. It's a societal ethical and moral standard that isn't laid out in writing, unless we're semantically talking about law, but is nonetheless understood. It isn't lawfully wrong to say rude things to someone for no reason, but we understand intrinsically that it isn't the **RIGHT** thing to do.

IT'S CONTAGIOUS

RIGHT is contagious. To that point, all behavior, good and bad, is contagious. That's kind of why I'm writing this book. Doing **RIGHT** by the world really does bring **RIGHT** back to you, especially when dealing with people. The "law of reciprocity," one of the strongest laws of human nature, is real. People will basically treat you in a manner similar to that which you treat them. And when you treat people **RIGHT**, it makes them feel

"RIGHT is contagious"

good and they feel obligated to treat you **RIGHT**, which makes you feel good right back. Think about kids. When we reinforce their good behavior, they are more likely to repeat that behavior.

This also works in the world around us. The world will basically send back to you what you put out in it. It's called the "law of attraction." When you are kind and decent and respectful to the world, the world will send that back to you. Yes, there are always exceptions to this rule, but when you give, treat, and do things in a certain way and when **RIGHT** is the base from which you're operating, it becomes contagious. It expands the circle. This program of action is for you, **RIGHT** is contagious for you. It makes you feel good and brings you good results. Those things will make you want to continue that behavior. Why wouldn't we want to perpetuate that behavior? Now think about your inner circle of family and closest friends. In the beginning, the people most likely to be influenced by **RIGHT** are those people in that inner circle. You can first build your influence of **RIGHT** with this inner circle.

THE MOST IMPORTANT PERSON IN THE WORLD

Success in life is about helping the person in front of you. "You will get all you want in life, if you help enough other people get what they want," wrote renowned speaker and author, Zig Ziglar. Far too often, we judge whether or not the person in front of us is going to be beneficial to our cause or purpose. We predetermine whether or not that person is going to be able to help us in some way or another, then we proceed to treat them as such. We should instead focus on that person and their wants and needs.

In the vast majority of cases, helping that person be successful will somehow contribute to our own success, even if you don't expect to see an impact at all. Following the path of mindfulness and staying in the moment, you know that the only person you can really help, besides yourself, in any given moment, is the person right in front of you. If you start focusing all your efforts on getting the most out of your interaction with the person in front of you, ALL of your relationships will be better. It's a cascade effect, a veritable waterfall of positivity. Your heightened since of attention will make people feel more valued by you. This in turn will make them want to be around you.

> "The most important person in the world is the person right in front of you"

Recently, I was on a date, enjoying a nice dinner and conversation. As we finished eating, we went and sat at the bar to talk some more. I know the owner of the restaurant, and she came over to greet us. I had always been friendly with Susan, but never had more than a superficial conversation with her. While we talked, she kept looking over at a group of people in the corner, with this warm, peaceful look on her face. After watching her for a moment, I realized that the two couples were somehow related to her.

"Are those your kids?" I asked, watching her response closely. She couldn't spit it out fast or proudly enough, "Yes, those are my sons," she said, beaming as she pointed at them, "and their wives. I just love my daughters-in-law."

She continued to gush. I could tell she was so happy to have some of her family there. "My son is a Marine, and he just got back from a tour in Afghanistan." You could see the tears that only a mother knows begin to well in her eyes. And at that moment, I made sure that she was the most important person in the world to me. I focused intently on what she was saying, our eyes locked in a stare of mutual admiration. I knew it would be a fleeting moment, but it was very special to Susan. These were her sons and the women that love them. These were some of the most important people in her life. These were the people she loved.

I said, "Wow, I come from a military family and I have great respect for everyone that serves. Please thank him for me for his service to our country." Wanting her to bask a little more in her moment, I asked one more question. "How happy and how proud are you?" She spent several minutes with joyful tears in her eyes and talked about how her son loved serving and being part of the Marines. She got to share what was valuable and significant to her. She will never forget that moment between us. I didn't care about the food or the wine, or my date for that matter. At that moment, I cared about Susan and the things she loved. And she could tell I was very sincere about it. We really need to just slow down and remember that the most important person in the world is the person sitting right in front of us. It doesn't matter who they are. They have their own emotions to share and unfortunately are sometimes not given the opportunity to do so. Everyone is valuable and significant in their own way and their own right.

HOPE IS RIGHT

Never deprive someone of hope; it might be all they have. Hope is the last thing to die! Hope is **RIGHT**. As long as there is hope, there are: dreams to conjure up, goals to achieve, love to find, friends to make, children to raise, fears to conquer, people to help, and a future to be had. Hope is a universal truth. Successful people have the ability to build up people's hopes. To help people birth new hope. And you have the responsibility to share hope when you have it. During the writing of my book, the OnFire Books team, Tiarra and Tammy, gave me hope during this process that I could complete my goals. We have so many opportunities to offer hope. As long as hope is alive, YOU are alive.

"As long as hope is alive, YOU are alive"

A good leader instills hope in their people. They are able to clearly show the team how their vision is going to be good for the team and the company (or family…it doesn't matter what group of people you are leading). A leader without followers is just a person out for a walk. If, as a leader, your vision isn't **RIGHT**, if it isn't good for the other people involved, no one is going to follow you. They may do what you tell them to because they have to, but they won't follow you wholeheartedly. You have to make sure that your people benefit from your vision, and that they want to grow with it. Leadership is nothing more than a transfer of feelings. A vision is a deep-seated feeling of what that person genuinely feels is the **RIGHT** way to do things in a given setting. Good leaders are able to get their people, be it family, employees, friends, or fellow church members to share in it. They are able to make people see that by sharing their vision, it's going to be good for them as well. You have to find what people love and help them get it. Where do your hopes align with the key people in your life and how can you help propel one another?

You cannot lead a group of people into doing something

or at least doing it well if you do not believe it yourself. Our beliefs are the strongest things in our lives. We live life based on those beliefs. And to see our people truly grow and do well, we have to truly believe in it ourselves. You must believe in it with all of your heart; otherwise you will not be able to convince them to believe in it. If they don't believe in it, they won't buy into it. In my trainings, I teach that the first sale you have to make is to make "them believe, that YOU BELIEVE, with all your heart." It's possible to transfer the wrong feelings, so you have to be sensitive enough to make sure you are transferring the **RIGHT** ones.

When mapping out the course of your life, the future you see is the future you get. What you repeatedly visualize in your perfect mind's eye slowly starts to manifest itself into your life. If you continually see yourself in successful situations, you will act in a way that helps create those successes. Mindfulness will help you to clarify your vision of your ideal self and circumstances in life. If you are hoping for realistic things, you have to be realistic. There has to be some measure of reality to that which we hope for. We have to apply **RIGHT** to hope. If I personally hope to be a superstar quarterback, that isn't going to happen. All of the details that are surrounding that thought are not **RIGHT**. Surround your hope with **RIGHT**, then you can see the future that you deserve and that you create around you.

From a very early age, I taught my children that they could do anything with their life that they truly set their minds to. They both really believe they can do just that. It is important to plant that seed in *everyone's* mind. "There's nothing I can't do. There are just things I haven't done yet." Even if I fail, it doesn't mean I can't achieve it. Failure doesn't define you; it

PREPARES you for the road that lies ahead. You've just eliminated one more of the potholes. After failing repeatedly with inventing the lightbulb, Albert Einstein famously said that he hadn't failed at all; he had just found hundreds of ways the light bulb wouldn't work. If you truly believe it with all your heart that you can do anything that is realistic, then you can. We have to remember what is **RIGHT** for us, what is appropriate for us, and what is realistic for us.

REFLECT AND RESPOND

1. What area in your life needs the most **RIGHT** attention?

2. What is the one **RIGHT** thing you can do today to start changing your life immediately and forever?

_____

_____

_____

_____

_____

_____

_____

_____

_____

_____

_____

_____

_____

PRINCIPLE 2
RESPECT? YOURSELF AND THE WORLD AROUND YOU

How do you define respect? Is it earned or is it a right afforded to everyone? And how do you **start at right** when it comes to respect? What's the **RIGHT** thing to do when someone is very obviously disrespecting you? Respect is a feeling of deep admiration for someone or something elicited by their abilities, qualities, or achievements. To me, respect is the foundation of all your good relationships and a lack of it can be the crumbling foundation of your bad relationships. Here's the catch-22. You can't give away something you don't have.

> "Respect can be like the air you breathe; you don't notice it until it's gone."

Respect starts with you. So, *starting at right* when it comes to respect means starting with you. If you don't respect yourself, how can you know how to respect other people or things? Self-respect or self-worth is the cornerstone of a healthy personality. You have to respect—that is, love—yourself before you can respect and love anyone else. And respect transcends people. It extends to respect for all life, respect for property, and respect for all things. You must respect yourself and the WORLD around you. That's everything you encounter, but it has to start with yourself. The most important voice that you listen to is your own. And the way you talk to yourself, ABOUT YOURSELF, is the key to having healthy self-respect.

Respect is also very contagious. When you treat other people with respect, they are far more likely to treat you with respect. Giving people their due respect will ingratiate them to you and a new relationship will start with a foundation of respectful reciprocity. In a sense, respect is like the air we breathe; you don't really notice it until it's not there anymore.

A great way to show respect is by really learning about people and what interests them. Go below the superficial level and really talk to your friends, your co-workers, and your close relatives…get the details about their daily interests and life. Find out what people LOVE and give it to them. In every relationship, in every business transaction, in every interaction between two people, it is important to remember that people are somewhat motivated by their own self-interest. If you start there and just genuinely help people achieve or acquire their own self-interest, or help them get what they love, then people will trust you and believe you. First comes respect… then comes trust…then comes love or mutual feelings. Help people get what they love, and they will love

> "First comes respect, then comes trust, then comes love or mutual feelings."

you. It's human nature.

That's the first step to building credibility, to people believing you, and believing in you. People believe what they see. They believe you really care about them when they see your genuine interest in their life and personal situations. It's an important initial step to really creating an emotional bond with them. And it has to be a genuine effort. You can't fake **RIGHT**. You have to be genuinely engaged in their interests, which just means you're knowledgeable about the details of their life: if they're married, have children, what their career is, and basic interests…things they love.

By using this approach and the age-old phenomenon of the "law of reciprocity" (which simply means people will treat you like you treat them), they will reciprocate the behavior. You will enhance the quality of your relationships. By helping people get the things they LOVE, it makes them feel good about you and their association with you. It makes them want to be around you, do business with you, be your friend, date you, love you, and be associated with you…it's just the **RIGHT** thing to do. When you impact things that are so important to them, it draws them closer to you.

If you want to find out what people love, follow their time and money. Follow the yellow brick road and it will lead you to a person's heart. In this instance, the yellow brick road represents two of the most valuable things a person has: their time and their money. Use your own life as an example. When you have spare time, void of any responsibility, what do you spend it doing? Dare I say your favorite hobby or pastime, quality time with your favorite people, or relaxing your favorite way? People spend their free time and money on the things and people they love and the things they deem **RIGHT** and important. It shows great respect for someone to make the effort to delve into their life and find the things they love. They will notice, and notch that into their memory bank of fond thoughts and feelings about you.

People speak with their money, or time, or friendship. You have heard the maxim, "people do business with people they know, like, and trust." They either reward your product and behavior and keep doing business with you, or keep being your friend, or they punish you and leave. In both of those examples, they are speaking with their money or their emotional currency; friendship or love. If someone has a bad experience with someone from a certain company, it can cause them to not do business with that company any longer. On the other hand, a positive experience—and especially a personal connection—can lead to a lifelong business relationship. And unfortunately, many times if there's a problem, you won't know about it until it's too late. People who choose to communicate their feelings in this manner don't usually talk to you about the circumstances surrounding the situation. You realize you lost a good customer when they don't reorder and avoid your calls. They speak with their money.

Do you remember who is the most important person in your life (remember Susan?)? The person sitting right in front of you. There were many times as a senior level executive that I was not so good at this. Oftentimes, I overlooked people, instead of really looking at the value that they bring as a human being. Too often, we get caught up in the trap of trying to determine how people can be good for us or what they can do for us. Who can move us along in our career? Who can help us climb the corporate ladder? Who can help us achieve a certain goal? We label their value to us by what we think they can do for us, when actually, research has proven that the happiest people are those that make a habit of giving, not getting. Give that person in front of you the respect they deserve as people, then watch how ALL PEOPLE work to the benefit of everyone around them. Here's what mindfulness teaches us about this whole person in front of you concept. If you are truly being mindful, which is the root of happiness, you can really only concentrate on one person, or one thing at a time. So, you might as well make the person in front of you the most important person in the world. They are the only one you can impact in that moment anyway.

"Good leaders show a genuine, personal interest in the people on their team"

As a leader, do you show a genuine interest (which is respect) in the people on your team and not just in the job they do? Do you put yourself in the position to genuinely engage with them to demonstrate that concern? Do they feel valued by you? Have you invested the time to show respect for that relationship? Remember, we spend time on that which we deem important. People quit people before they quit companies, partnerships, or relationships. Customers, co-workers, and others relate with people first, then they will relate to a company. Someone will leave their job because they don't get along with their boss or other co-workers that they must work closely with. They can be happy with the company and what it stands for, but if they are unhappy with the people they work closest with, it can still cause them to leave. It all comes back to respect.

ACTIVE LISTENING

A major key to showing respect in our interactions with others and creating a positive experience is listening. The benefits of being a good listener are long established. Listening is an active sport. You must, as Joe Girard, the greatest salesman in the world as listed in *Guinness World Records,* says, "Listen with your whole face." When asked what he meant by this, Joe elaborated, "Your expression has to show people you care; open stance, eye contact, head slightly tilted to one side, face and forehead

> **"When people say something to you, it means something to them. SO LISTEN"**

going up in an attentive posture…in other words, having a receptive and welcoming look about you." When people say something to you, IT MEANS SOMETHING TO THEM! So, LISTEN. A great example of this is a story about my daughter, Tori. I'll never forget the sound of her voice when, at nine or ten years old, she said with a very aggravated tone, "Daddy, listen with your face!" She was telling me a story (I don't even remember about what, but I sure remember that tone), and I was trying to do something else and also listen to her. So, I was looking away, and said, "I'm listening, baby." Well, she didn't buy that for a second. Even at such a young age, she knew better. You aren't truly listening to someone, and thus respecting their view or opinion, if you are also trying to do something else. Her comment, in essence, said "No Daddy, you're not listening TO me, if you're not looking AT me." Out of the mouths of babes. We tend to assign our own meaning to the value of what people are saying. Instead, we should try to listen to UNDERSTAND instead of listening to RESPOND. By taking the time and interest to listen carefully to other people, it shows that we care about their opinions. And, it's the ultimate sign of respect to put their interests before our own. If we listen to understand, we are better able to help that person.

Assumptions have the power to color our entire perception of a situation, or a person. It's a natural human instinct to make assumptions about most things that come across our paths, but assumptions should be undertaken from a place of **RIGHT** and from the wisdom of past experiences. Always assume positive intent. It makes you see the brighter side of life and people. It is a great sign of respect to always assume that people mean well in the things they do. If a person says or does something that may seem a little off-color or out of place, if you will assumethat this person means no ill will or bad intention, it makes it easier for you to overlook or forgive that person. Why? Most people may not understand how something said off the cuff or done in the moment can be received. This is especially true in the digital age where texting is so prevalent. In the written word, it is easy to lose tone and intention and thus, the true meaning of someone's message may not be clear. It becomes easier to read the wrong thing into their message.

We've all been in that situation where something happens and we say, "That's not what I meant," or "You took that the wrong way." "We judge ourselves by our intentions, and others by their behavior," as Stephen M.R. Covey wrote in *The Speed of Trust*. We know what we mean when we say or do something. But too often, our intentions get overshadowed by our actions. People believe what they see, so they believe our actions more than our words. And one of our most important actions is how we listen.

One of the most important things we can give another person is our UNDIVIDED ATTENTION. This is a way of communicating to another person that they matter, and that they are important and significant. By making the person in front of you the most important person, you might as well make them feel good. You might as well invest the time in them. This brings you back to mindfulness. By giving that person in front of you all of you, they will give you all of themselves back. Along with this gift, we give people one of the most valuable feelings a person can have, that of being/feeling significant. It makes all people feel important when we entrust our most treasured asset, our time, to them. Research also proves that those who have deep emotional connections with as many people as possible live a more fulfilling life.

The ultimate respect is putting the wants and needs of others before your own. One word for this is "altruism." And think about the media phenomenon that has become so popular in the last few years: MILITARY HOMECOMINGS. Who can watch a military father or mother who's been on tour in Afghanistan for twelve months surprise their kids at a school assembly, and not get a tear in their eye? It's because we all know that "freedom isn't free." Someone has made huge sacrifices of time and personal safety so that the rest of us can be safe and free. And human nature has proven that when you help other people, they feel obligated to help you in return. It is also true that helping the people closest to you (spouse, friend, sibling, or co-worker) get what they want will very directly help you. Example: Your boss wants to hit the department's sales goals for the quarter. When you help him hit the sales goal and get what he wants, you get more sales and probably more commissions. You then get a high mark from your boss for hitting your personal sales goal, and the company does better, thus ensuring that you have a job. So, by ensuring that your boss got what he wanted, to hit a sales goal, it also helped you get what you want: recognition, more money, self-confidence in hitting a goal, and maybe most importantly, the good feeling we all get when we help someone.

"An attitude of gratitude helps keep your life in perspective"

One thing that really helps us keep our lives in perspective is "the attitude of gratitude." Melody Beattie is quoted as saying, "Gratitude unlocks the fullness of life. It turns what we have into enough, and more. It turns denial into acceptance, chaos into order, confusion into clarity…Gratitude makes sense of our past, brings peace for today, and creates a vision for tomorrow." This is all about respecting yourself and brings respecting yourself full circle, for when you become **RIGHT** minded and focus on helping other people, you invariably encounter people that are less fortunate than yourself. When you see some of the conditions that other people live through, you may gain a deeper appreciation for the good things in your life, things that you may take for granted.

Another thing I teach in my sales seminars, that very directly relates to respect, is the "touch factor." I always say, "You have to touch people here (and I put my hand on my heart) before you try and touch them here (and I turn around so the audience can see me grabbing my wallet)." This very simple analogy refers to being more concerned about the customer and what they want than about yourself and making the sale. I teach that "sales is nothing more than helping people get what they want." And if you genuinely put the client's interest first, and if you sincerely help them get what they love (reference to the heart), then you will make the sale and get what you want (the wallet, money). And starting at the heart most always leads to the wallet anyway because people can sense that you have their best interest in mind. When we as leaders are trying to motivate our people, we need to first keep in mind how that which we're trying to accomplish may also be good for them, and how it will touch their hearts. Is it something they love? Is accomplishing this goal good for the team? The company that approaches employees from the wallet standpoint, looking at them from a purely monetary perspective, often misses the opportunity to help that individual grow as a person and thus as a teammate. When they grow, the company grows. People respond better when they know that the company, that YOU, care about them first, then the project or sale.

"Touch their heart before you ever try to touch their wallet"

Why is that important? Because it can seem hard to find people's hearts in the business world, but they're there. If you have an office, you may spend almost more time there than anywhere else in life. Think about your office and the things you have put on the walls and desk. Chances are you've surrounded yourself with things that mean something to you: pictures of your family, pets, hobbies, and maybe vacations… important things in your life. Remember this: pay attention to what people love when you walk into their office. Take a moment and start from the left and look around their office walls. That is their space. People like to be proud of the space they spend a lot of time in. Halfway around the room, nod your head a couple of times, and make a short comment like "Wow, that looks interesting." Then look the rest of the way around the walls. The things they love will be proudly displayed on their office walls. Lastly, look at their desk. The things or people they love the most will be on their desk because they are the closest things to them. This is the power of observation at its finest.

Make it a point to mention and make small talk about the things you notice. This will be an immediate ice breaker and endear you to them. To truly be effective and wow the people in your life, take a moment later to record all the things that are important to that client, friend, acquaintance, or teammate. Don't rely on memory. Start a spreadsheet of important clients, close friends, new friends, church friends, etc. and record that important information about the person. And when you know in advance that you'll be seeing that person, study that information. Walk in and ask your client how their child is doing. Refer to their child by name. Your client will firstly be impressed that you remembered his child's name, and secondly feel very significant that you cared enough to remember personal information about them and what is important to them.

I can give you an example of this phenomenon from my own experience. In this instance, my team was looking to establish a new relationship with a large, successful company, and I went in to meet our perspective client, and set a meeting with their purchasing agent. In my meeting with Melissa, I did exactly the exercise I mentioned earlier. She had pictures of cats on her desk. I brought up that I loved Siamese cats and the fact that I had one myself. We spent an hour talking about cats, then I took her to lunch and found out that she was dating a new man named Chris. I took notes and when I called her later, I was able to go over those notes, and I knew how to talk to her. Six months later, that diligence and discipline got us all of that company's business.

By caring more about her, touching her in her heart first, we were able to touch that company's wallet. But you have to have the daily discipline to write these things down for later use.

Management isn't about walking around seeing if people are in their office working. It's about creating conditions for people to do their best work and enjoy personal growth. Research proves that personal development is very high on the list of priorities for employees. An atmosphere of respect and the ability to learn and grow is important to keeping talented people. To get the most out of others, you need to GIVE the best of yourself—great leaders lead by example. They lead from the front. Success breeds success. When your people, be it family, friends, or co-workers, see you giving the best of yourself, they are far more likely to follow your example, rather than your words. Good leaders display the type of character they want their company to follow. Good leaders **start at right**, then expect the rest of their teams to do the same. But with that expectation, they also give them the proper training and tools to accomplish the **RIGHT** standard they have set.

> "To get the most out of others, you need to GIVE the best of yourself—great leaders lead by example"

If people like you, they will listen to you. But if they trust you, they will follow you. Trust is a firm belief in the reliability, truth, ability, or strength of someone or something. Respect and trust go hand in hand and are the foundations of good leadership. People have to believe in you, what you stand for, and what you're trying to get them to stand for. If they have that belief, that trust, they will do whatever you require of them. That is the ultimate show of respect.

It is easy to be likeable. You can do that almost instantly with people just by being kind and showing them attention. To have them follow you, however, they must truly believe in you and what you stand for. First comes respect, then comes trust, and then comes love (or another display of caring)…in that order. That's how people work.

How can you show the kind of respect for others and the world around you that inspires them to believe in you and what you are doing? Make this a priority in your personal life first, extend it to your professional life, and sit back and enjoy the life you've always dreamed of.

REFLECT AND RESPOND

1. What is the one thing you can STOP DOING TODAY that will show more respect to yourself?

2. Who is the one person you should show more respect to? And how can you accomplish that?

3. What are the two to three things you can change about your behavior/character that will make people feel more respected by you?

PRINCIPLE 3
TAKE? RESPONSIBILITY

What do you take on as your responsibility? Is there a clear definition of how to **start at right** when it comes to being responsible?

Jeffrey Gitomer has said, "Successful people take responsibility for everything they do and everything that happens to them." People understand that if they do something, they are responsible for it. The second part of this statement is the part that most people have trouble accepting because we don't want to take responsibility for things we can't control.

Does anyone want to be the one to stop the speeding train they may not have even known was on the track? Especially if they weren't the one to disengage the brakes? To many people, this seems wrong and almost unfair. People can see taking responsibility for the things that they do, but not necessarily the things that happen to them.

"Successful people take responsibility for everything they do and everything that happens to them"

You can't help the fact that you got laid off because the company downsized. How are you responsible for that? You technically can't control that, but you are responsible for how you respond. You are responsible for your life. You are responsible for how you handle the things that happen to you, whether it is a decision you made or a condition that you endured. The condition in the case of being laid off is still a choice. If you respond with the mentality that life isn't fair, that you never get a break, you'll continue to allow your conditions to control your destiny, instead of your decisions. Everything from that moment forward will be impacted by the way you respond. That means that layoff can affect you well into the foreseeable future. But you can be responsible for that situation and go out and find another job. You may take a twenty-four-hour pity party and then you are going to shake it off and make it your job to find a new job. You can make sure you're not a victim of the circumstances. No more excuses...it doesn't matter what happens. Successful people take responsibility for everything in their lives. This is the perfect example of a "meet me in the mirror" moment. This is when you look yourself squarely in the eyes and say, "You've got this, Brian Faught. Come on... go conquer your world...let's go!!!" You give your absolutely best pep talk and then you go "conquer your world." You've got this!

FAILURE

You have not failed until you quit. Failure doesn't define you. Failure teaches you. A person can get discouraged many times, but he is not a failure until he begins to blame somebody else and stops trying. He has not failed until he actually quits. Failure is learning. Failure is one bad decision or bad break closer to success. Failure defines a situation, NOT YOU. Failure is what happened to you in that particular event or effort; it's not who you are.

When I left my old company, my partner and I were going to try and get into the medical marijuana business in a big way. My partner owned and operated another company, so I was running the building of this new cannabis business. I spent fourteen hours a day working on building this company. I had never worked harder on anything in my life. I hired some of the best people in the cannabis industry to help me so that I could make sure I was doing everything **RIGHT**. My goal was to put myself in the best position possible to get the cannabis licenses that were soon to be awarded by the state of Arkansas. "No stone left unturned" was my daily motto for eighteen months. I had a purchase agreement to buy land from the city of Fayetteville, AR, to build a cannabis cultivation facility, and had to go before the city council to get approval for the contingent offer. These city council meetings are televised, so my efforts wound up on TV, and in a lot of newspapers throughout the state of Arkansas, and I ended up getting a lot of exposure from this event. Everyone who was supporting me thought I had a very good chance of getting the license. I also did several things that I was told other applicants weren't doing. Well, to make a long story short, I didn't get that license and I was devastated. There was so much disappointment. I had failed at something I had worked so hard for. And because of the media exposure, it was a very public failure. Have you had a moment where you failed and it felt like that sucker punch to the stomach? It can be easy for us to fall into thinking we failed because we weren't good enough.

But that failure doesn't define me and yours doesn't define you. That was just one event in my life. It doesn't define who I am, and it doesn't define where I am in this life. I got countless emails and calls reminding me of just that. I texted several of the winners and congratulated them for their hard work and success.

That failure was just part of God's plans for me. I did end up getting one of the medical marijuana dispensary licenses, so my efforts weren't completely in vain. But the big prize, the cultivation facility, slipped through my fingers. That failure was a condition.

> "Failure doesn't define you; it teaches you"

And I long ago made the decision to move past that and continue my other lines of work, which now included a medical marijuana dispensary. This was my plan B. I've always taught my kids that you have to have a plan B in life. Plan A doesn't always work, and the successful person ALWAYS knows what their next move, their Plan B, is. It's the responsible thing to do. That's how you keep failures from completely disrupting your life. If you always have a backup plan, you're never left without hope. Your back is never truly against the wall. These are the things, the decisions, that separate successful people from the rest of the pack. So, part of starting at **RIGHT** when it comes to being responsible is having a very workable plan B at the ready at all times.

MAXIMIZE YOUR POTENTIAL

A very important point to remember for all people in a position of responsibility is to "Only do what only you can do." As a leader, only do what only you can do and delegate the rest. It's our responsibility as leaders to make sure our talent is maximized to its fullest potential. Typically, that means doing things at a senior level that require a highly sophisticated skill set. It's your responsibility to not get bogged down in daily details that can be handled by someone else on your team. The learning experience will be good for your teammates, while freeing you up for the things required of someone in your position. Be a leader, not a manager. You can't do everything. Don't do someone else's job if it takes you away from completing what only you can do. You have to let it go and let people make their decisions and do their job so that you can do yours. Everyone can work better and do better when they are doing the things that only they can do. Those are the areas of your strength. Focus on this and teach your team to do the same. If everyone is working on things associated with their giftedness, then they are probably doing things they enjoy. When people do what they enjoy and are good at, they typically do it well and with a greater sense of pride and accomplishment. They will also put in the extra effort to get it RIGHT when doing the things they love.

What else are you doing by delegating these tasks? You are building your team's confidence and self-esteem, you are giving them the experience to be a good teammate, and you are being a good leader by letting them do the things that only they can do. It helps us maximize the full potential of our teams and ourselves.

WORK ON BECOMING

Expand your horizons by BECOMING; becoming a better

friend, becoming a better spouse, becoming a better co-worker, becoming a better person, becoming a better leader, and becoming a more well-rounded individual. Always work on becoming, growing, and getting better. If we don't continue to "become" a better person, a better spouse, a better leader, and a better teammate, then our talent level, our skill set which makes us unique and different, slowly starts to erode. When we are always becoming, we are always growing.

> **"Everything that stops growing slowly starts to die"**

The opposite of living isn't just dying, it's also stagnation. That which stands still for too long often becomes too set in its mold to break free. Think of a fresh glass of water that will become murky over time or a bolt that rusts because it's never turned.

Develop a lifelong student mentality. In nature, everything that stops growing slowly starts to die. The same thing happens with people. When we stop learning, we start to die "in place," meaning that we won't expand beyond the place we find ourselves in at that particular time in our lives. "In place" is that current position you have at work, the current state of your marriage, and your current financial situation. The only way to change "your place" in life is to do something different. Learn a new skill set at work, read a book about the things that are important to your mate, or attend a seminar about effective communication. Do something or learn something new.

To truly change your life, you have to change the things you do daily. Start an exercise regiment, take the first thirty minutes of the day as a time to meditate and read a devotional, or set aside thirty minutes a day for quality one-on-one time with your spouse or children. Do something different TODAY… something that takes some discipline. Discipline is like **RIGHT**; it's CONTAGIOUS! When discipline helps you get better in one area of your life, it's very easy to spread that feeling, that success, into other areas. Do it…now, today, because you can, because you have to, and because the better you is counting on you to deliver. If you stop growing, you start dying.

There are centuries-old trees that have robustly grown to majestic heights. But these trees have finite days of growing. When that growth stops, that is when they slowly start to die, rotting from the inside out and crashing to the forest floor. This is what happens to people also. People get to a certain place in their life and in their career where they become satisfied. They've reached their goal. They've accomplished their dream or what they set out to do. When they reach that place, very often, they ease off the gas. They've made it. They can relax a little, and finally take it easy.

It's been said that we typically get 10 percent higher or lower than the place, the goal that we've set for ourselves. "If I can just get to $100,000 a year income, I'll be satisfied." Then, we hit that milestone and that's where a lot of people stop. They've made it. They've hit their goals…they've arrived. But you can't stop learning or becoming. Yes, it's a slow process, oftentimes going completely unnoticed. It's a silent killer. You have to keep getting better AT SOMETHING. Learning is contagious. Learning is **RIGHT**. Getting better…growing, is contagious. If you ever stop doing the things that got you where you're at, that's when you start to "die in place."

This is our responsibility as a parent as well. As my children get older, and I have grandchildren, I have had to learn a new place for myself. When my daughter, Tori, got married, I had to learn that I was no longer the most important male figure in her life. And that is the way it should be. It's my responsibility to help teach her and coach her about how to be a great wife. One day when she was pregnant, and on bed rest feeling horrible, she was snapping at her husband, Brian. Despite the fact that she was miserable and uncomfortable, I said. "Darling, I know you feel bad, but it's not his fault." And the words hadn't left my mouth when she shot back, "Yea Dad, it kind of is his fault. He helped get me this way." And to that, I calmly sat down and minded my own business. Point being though, it's my responsibility to teach my daughter the things a good man looks for in a wife. And I take that very seriously.

HAPPINESS

We are responsible for our own happiness. **We just are. And don't let anyone try and tell you otherwise.** Happiness studies show that experiences increase contentment far more than things. We can't depend on things, we can't depend on other

> "Happiness is a BE, not a WHEN. It's a decision, not a condition"

people, and we can't depend on conditions. We are responsible for the happiness we want and deserve in life. Happy is a state of being. Far too often, we make happy a "when." I'm going to be happy "when" I get a new car...I'm going to be happy "when" I meet the man of my dreams...I'm going to be happy "when" I get a promotion. The problem with making happy a "when" is "when" never truly comes. "When" is a condition, and when we make a "when a condition" the root of our happiness, and when that "when" is finally achieved or received, we just find another "when" to attach our happiness to. We replace one "when" with the next "when." We've trained ourselves to relate happiness to a condition, a "when." It's a never-ending cycle of seeking, but not fully enjoying, and not ever reaching satiation.

Happiness is a "be." I'm going to "be" happy. It's an attitude, a decision. When you wake up every morning, you get to make the decision that you're going to be happy. You're going to reflect and focus on the positive things in your life. You're going to put your attitude of gratitude on full display for the world (and yourself) to see. By making happiness a decision, a "be," you're not allowing any conditions to affect that state of being happy. Research has proven that experiences with other people (people believe what they see) are far more rewarding to people than purchases or things. Giving and receiving gifts is an experience. But it's the experience of that act you created that generates the happiness, not the gift itself.

We either make ourselves miserable or we make ourselves happy and strong. The amount of work is the same, the energy we use is the same. This comes back to how you talk to yourself. If you're unhappy, change the way you talk to yourself. The quality of your life is between your ears. It has to do with the attitude you cultivate, like the attitude of gratitude. I won't let things make me miserable. It is a decision and my responsibility to have these situations and events in my life make

> "We either make ourselves miserable or we make ourselves happy and strong. The amount of work is the same."

me strong. But still, like everyone else, negative thoughts will creep into my mind and it's up to me to alter those thoughts. You can instantly change your mood by changing which voice you are listening to in your head. We can either listen to the voice of positive affirmation and gratitude telling us I can do it, I'm a success, I am talented and capable, and I am blessed to have a great job and many people that love me. Or, we can listen to the voice of self-doubt and self-pity telling us my boss isn't fair with me, I never get good breaks, life isn't fair, why did my marriage fail, and why can't I find the **RIGHT** mate. It's our choice and responsibility to control the voice in our head.

I do motivational speaking and despite that fact, every now and then, I have to stop myself and say, "This is not who I am." I can take that situation and have it make me strong, or I can allow it to whittle away at my self-confidence and create anxiety and negativity in my life. What voice are you listening to? Is it the voice of self-doubt or the voice of success? Invest where you'd like to receive a return. Invest in the positive and affirming. The cost is exactly the same, but the results are vastly different.

"Motion creates emotion... so smile"

Did you know that motion creates emotion? Smile and see how that affects your immediate countenance. Go for a brisk walk and see how that immediately makes you feel better. Start working on a project you've been putting off and see how that immediately makes you feel more competent and confident in your work and makes you willing to take on other tasks.

Recently, I was going to meet some clients in Florida to play golf, and decided I needed to get some practice in. I went to the driving range and hit some balls, and the pollen and heat of the day exhausted me. I went home feeling like I wanted to call off the rest of the day. I was scheduled to go to the gym with some buddies that evening and was on the brink of canceling. Even on the drive to the gym I was on the verge of calling and telling them I wasn't going to make it. But I pushed through, and when I walked into the gym and saw my buddies, they all greeted me and we started our usual friendly banter. I instantly felt better. Just going through the motions of getting in there changed my mood. I got through that first exercise set and I felt great, instantly better. More confident, more energized, and more happy. There are certain things every day that we all dread the most. Do those things first and it will empower you for the rest of the day!

START WITH THE TRUTH

We have to take responsibility and acknowledge things as they are, not as we want them to be. We believe what we tell ourselves over and over. And if we repeatedly tell ourselves, "It's not my fault" then we start to believe that. We can create our own illusion of truth by repeatedly telling ourselves something. An illusion of truth is something we say over and over (either to ourselves or others) that could conceivably be true. A good example of this phenomenon is when I was training young salespeople for the DIRECTV industry. I would coach them to say over and over, "Sir, you're

> "An illusion of truth is something you say over and over that could conceivably be true"

going to LOVE the DIRECTV DVR." I knew that most TV buffs actually do love having a DVR. And the DIRECTV DVR was known in the industry as being one of the best. So, it was in fact conceivably true that a potential new customer would "LOVE the DIRECTV DVR." By repeatedly saying this to customers, we were creating this illusion of truth that became a powerful tool in closing sales. The more they said it, the more the customers believed it. The more the customers believed it, the more systems they sold.

When I was trying to build my cannabis business, I created my own illusion of truth about that business. I told myself over and over, "I'm going to get these licenses and I'm going to be hugely successful in the medical cannabis industry." I was building my own illusion of truth for myself and the people who would work for me. Conceivably, it was true. I thought I was doing things that most other applicants weren't doing. I created that illusion of truth in my mind and failure seemed impossible to me. But when I failed, I had to let it go.

We've all heard the phrase "talk is cheap." It's easy to say what we're going to do. But backing up those words with actions is sometimes vastly harder. The Bible says, "Faith without works is dead." We can say we will work hard, we can say we believe, and we can say all the RIGHT things and buy time. Until we validate what we say with works, people, our people, are going to be hesitant or even be skeptical. Once when my daughter was very young, I was taking her to school one morning—I was divorced from her mother and had joint custody—and she had left her homework at her mother's house. Tori took school very seriously and was concerned about making sure we got her work, which was due that day. The night before I had told her that we would call her mother and make sure she dropped the material off at school.

Well, that morning when we called, Tori became upset about the possibility that her mother might forget. She ran her own very successful business, and at times, got pulled away by her busy schedule. Her mother told us on the phone that she would bring it. But when we got off the phone, I looked at my daughter and she had tears streaming down her face. She said, "Daddy, Mommy gets busy and she may not get my homework there when I need it. I know she'll bring it, but I have to make sure I have it now." She had to see it. People believe what they see. So, we drove straight to her mother's house and picked up her homework (which was already in her car to be taken to school). But the point was, Tori had to see the works.

People believe what you do.

PRIORITIES

You've heard it said that many times in life you will face the pain of discipline or the pain of regret. The choice is yours. Life can be full of pain…if we let it be. It's our responsibility to make time to do the things that are important in our lives. People do what they're scheduled to do, and they schedule what's important. Approach pain from a decision standpoint, not a reaction or condition standpoint. Your responsibility is to make sure that if there will be pain, that you take responsibility to make a choice to use the pain of discipline instead of the pain of regret. They both cause the same pain. You choose if you will discipline yourself to reach your goals, or endure the pain of failure. I took the pain of discipline when I initially failed at cannabis, and I pushed it into my real legacy and poured it into *The Power of Right* and writing this book. I knew that I did not want to die with this part of my legacy left to perish with me.

I love the old saying, "The lazy man works twice." Either TAKE the time to do it **RIGHT** the first time or MAKE the time to do it again. Take the responsibility to do it **RIGHT** the first time or you will spend lots of time doing it again. You have to adhere to *the power of right*. There is almost always a **RIGHT** way to do everything. In 90 percent of the situations you face, someone has already experienced that same situation, or something extremely close to it. The **RIGHT** way to handle it has been established for the most part. Maybe you need to research the way to handle a situation the first time. Save time and effort. Do it **RIGHT** the first time. The lazy man works twice. These are situations where starting at **RIGHT** really will pay off in everything you do.

> "Be obsessed with something good: reading, learning, smiling, laughing, loving, teaching... anything that moves you forward in life"

Learn to be obsessed with something good in life, i.e., exercising, helping people, reading, learning, singing, loving, smiling, or anything good and productive. Obsession breeds passion...passion comes from the heart...whatever comes from the heart is what you genuinely believe in. Everyone is good at something, and maybe even obsessed and good at something. But you have to be careful with what you choose to be obsessed about.

You have to be obsessed with doing the **RIGHT** thing. Remember, when **RIGHT** gets on you, it becomes a behavior. But when **RIGHT** gets in you,it becomes your identity. Starting at **RIGHT** will help you discover your true passion in life. Then you'll find yourself gravitating toward people who are passionate about the same things. Obsession is the spice of life. It is the thing that cannot be taken away from you, and that fire that can never be put out. I am obsessed with *The Power of Right*, and have been working on it for more than twelve years. I have invested countless amounts of time and money in this program. You are reading this book because I am passionate and obsessed with changing your life with *The Power of Right*.

REFLECT AND RESPOND

1. What area of your life are you struggling to take responsibility for?

2. How can you be more intentional about taking responsibility in other areas of your life?

_____

_____

_____

_____

_____

_____

_____

_____

_____

_____

_____

_____

PRINCIPLE 4
CONSIDER? THE CONSEQUENCES OF YOUR ACTIONS

You can tell how important something is today by measuring the potential future impact it will have on your life. You can either think something into happening or allow it to happen. It's your choice. This is the ultimate think it to happen question. Of all the questions in this program, this one really makes you think past the initial queue. This one question could literally determine the success or failure of your entire life. By utilizing *The Power of Right* technique, you are giving yourself a split second to really Consider? what is this action, this thought, or this conversation going to cost you or do for you? This is the prime example of your decisions or your conditions determining your future. If you stop and Consider? you are thinking it to happen. You are giving yourself a chance to respond instead of reacting. You are making a decision that will have some impact on your future, your destiny. If you just react to your circumstances, you are allowing it to happen.

You are reacting, and thus allowing your conditions to determine your future.

Dr. Edward Banfield of Harvard University discovered that one of the major reasons for success in life was a particular attitude of the mind. Banfield called this attitude "long time perspective." Time perspective referred to how far you projected into the future

"One of the greatest indicators of future success in people is their ability to have long time perspective"

when you decided what you were going to do or not do in the present. He said that men and women who were the most successful in life and the most likely to move up economically were those who took the future into consideration with every decision they made in the present. Consider? How does this decision stand the test of time? What consequence, good or bad, will accompany it? What's the consequence of acting or not acting on it? Consider...think...decide! Talk about *starting at right*! This question is one of the anchors of the program, and may be one of the most beneficial to you and your team.

There is an ancient Chinese proverb that says, "Dig the well before you are thirsty." The Chinese have had it **RIGHT** for centuries. Consider the power of water. We need it for our livestock, for ourselves, and for our land. Why wouldn't you consider that you need to be working on this? This ancient proverb warns us of the penalties for not considering? What's the consequence of not digging the well? Death by dehydration? What's the consequence of not preparing adequately for that job assignment? Getting fired? Think of the difference it could make if you would just stop and ask yourself that one question: Consider?

People don't change any behavior until they become disturbed enough by the consequences of that behavior. Do you know anyone that has ever stopped smoking cigarettes? Ask them how long they smoked, if they ever thought about quitting but didn't, and what made them finally quit. In most all cases, they didn't quit until the consequence of smoking became greater than the consequence of quitting. Your child doesn't clean their room until you threaten to (or actually do) take away their phone, car, or other privileges. Change comes when we change our perspective in order to see the consequences of our actions.

"Change the way you look at things, and the things you see will change"

If you change the way you look at things, the things you see will change. Perception is reality in the vast majority of our interactions with people. Their perception is our reality. Consider how things would be if you had just _____! You fill in the blank.

- Considered the feelings of my spouse.

- Considered the point of view of my co-worker.

- Considered the effects of my actions on my neighbor.

- Considered my investment in my future.

- What else might you have considered?

Stopping and considering the perspective of others will change your life. Consider that. If you changed the way you perceived a particular situation, if you considered your teammate's point of view, if you really listened to what your spouse wanted, or if you just changed the way you looked at the facts...would it change what you actually see regarding that situation? Chances are it would. Life is about perspective. And in most cases, someone else's perspective about a particular situation is OUR REALITY concerning them and that circumstance. So many times, if we change the way we look at things, we can actually begin to see things like others do and find some sort of common ground. "Walk a mile in their shoes," and your communication with people will greatly improve.

Once I was traveling to Florida for a seminar and my connection was in Atlanta. They announced the boarding process and I got up and stood in line. Just as they were about to start boarding the plane, the desk attendant came over the loudspeaker and said that phrase we all dread hearing, "Ladies and gentlemen, I'm sorry to announce that there will be a short delay in our departure. Maintenance has discovered a minor issue that must be fixed before we can leave." You could feel and hear the collective groan from the waiting passengers.

I'm the best flyer on the planet because I never allow the conditions surrounding my travel to affect my attitude. My only requirement for a good flight is that I walk off the plane in an upright position. So, I just started looking around for a store to get a snack. As I was looking, I noticed the lady beside me really getting agitated. She had called someone on the phone and was pitching a fit about the delay. She hung up and looked at me, saying, "Can you believe this? It always happens to me. Every time I fly, there's always a problem." I

"Look at the way things COULD be" said, "Well, ma'am, wouldn't you rather they find that problem down here, than up there?" as I pointed to the sky. She got the funniest look on her face and said, "Well, I never thought of it like that," and her mood instantly changed. I laughed and told her, "You can thank me later."

Look at the way things COULD be. People believe what they see. Picture in your perfect mind's eye the perfect outcome of whatever it is you want. Look at the way things could be, instead of how they are. Speak to things in the manner you want them to occur. The things you continually think about and speak about are the things that slowly start to manifest themselves in your life. As you speak about something in the present tense, like it's already happened, your mind and body begin to accept that as a reality. Your subconscious mind is literal...it believes exactly what you tell it. You begin to believe those words and act on those words, and slowly bring those words to fruition...bring them to life. What you think about, you will speak about. What you speak about, you will bring about. This is the whole premise behind "meet me in the mirror," and practicing out loud. Starting your day with positive affirmations from the most important person in the world, YOU, sets the tone for your attitude for the rest of the day. Please, please, please, "MEET ME IN THE MIRROR" and start changing your life TODAY!

A hunch is **RIGHT** trying to tell you something. In my earlier horse racing story, I had a hunch the cashier had paid me too much money...I was **RIGHT**. Be still, listen to that still small voice inside you. The very action/prompting/response of a question is enough to make you stop for a split second and,

Consider? **RIGHT** is a powerful presence in your life. When you get committed to following **RIGHT**, being **RIGHT**, seeking **RIGHT**, celebrating **RIGHT**, and most importantly, **STARTING AT RIGHT**, you get better at listening to **RIGHT**. You begin to recognize it when it makes itself evident. You don't question things that you used to question. They just seem **RIGHT**.

You take as true things that follow the vein of **RIGHT**. The world is telling you what **RIGHT** is. You just have to stop the noise, stop the chaos, and stop the indecision…you just have to Be Still, and listen. You have to be listening to get out of your own way. The Bible says, "Be still, and know that I am God." He's telling us to get out of the way, be still. He's got this…He created the original **RIGHT** for us all to follow. Get out of the way and let your mind and body do what it knows to be right. Let right be the starting point of everything you do. Be still and know that starting at **RIGHT** is never wrong.

"A hunch is RIGHT trying to tell you something"

How many times have you heard the phrase, "Going out on a limb?" It is used to describe doing something that may be dangerous or risky. What if success is on the other side of risky? I challenge you to go out on a limb…just don't take a saw with you. Give yourself a chance to succeed. Consider: Does this decision put me out on a limb? If I want decisions to control my destiny, am I boxing myself into a boring life? Am I ever going to take any risks? Am I ever going to have any fun? The saw is your own self-doubt and the voices of other people who say, "That is going to be too much work, that's going to be too hard, or that goes against the grain of anything you've ever done." You have to go out on a limb, but you don't take those doubts, those negative thoughts with you on that limb. I know that people will benefit by incorporating this into their lives. To truly grow, to rise to the level of achievement that you want for yourself, YOU MUST go out on a limb every now and then.

THE POWER OF OBSERVATION

Want to know what to do in a particular situation? Just look around. What you're thinking about doing, what you're considering, has been done many times before. The answer is out there; you just have to find it. You don't have to reinvent the wheel. Learn to harness the power of observation. You don't have to read a book to learn. Think about the power of seeing what is out there already; people believe what they see. I drive past a tire shop every day on my way out of town, but I never really saw it. It wasn't something I needed, so I wasn't looking for it. I never observed something that was right in front of me. So, when I needed to get new tires, I wondered where a tire shop was. I then did what we all do when we need something. I googled tire shops in my town and low and behold, there it was…four minutes from my house. Now, I think about the fact that I can learn more by being observant, watching people, noticing my surroundings, and just listening.

"An important thing in communication is to hear what isn't being said."

An important thing in communication is to hear what isn't being said. Considering what isn't being said is important to you because it can help you figure out how to move forward. If you're in a business negotiation, and you know that this particular client has been price-sensitive in other areas, you can correctly assume that they will be price-sensitive in this situation as well. But they haven't said a thing about price in this case. Beware of the elephant in the room and factor that into your final proposal. When you're considering the consequences of your own actions, you have to take into account the actions and interests of others. Everything has a cause and effect. And watching people, studying people, really listening to what they're saying and NOT saying can have a huge impact on your decisions and their consequences. It is said that upwards of 80 percent of communication is nonverbal; it's tone, body language, and facial expressions. Getting good at understanding those forms of communication will help bosses, co-workers, friends, or spouses fill in the gaps. What isn't being said with a word may very well be said through a furrowed brow and crossed arms. Always consider what isn't being said. Observe and be mindful.

And now, consider this…Wherever you are in life, at this moment in time, is exactly where you DESERVE to be. Ouch, I know that sucks to hear sometimes. Your place in life is a result of the decisions you have made, and the actions that followed those decisions. That is a tough pill to swallow at times, for all of us. Four years ago, I was fifty-five years old, in the middle of a divorce, and losing more than half of my net worth and the lifestyle that I had enjoyed for many, many years. It was hard to

> "Wherever you are in life, at this moment in time, is exactly where you DESERVE to be."

hear myself say that I deserved to be in that position. But I had to consider the consequences of my actions. I was obviously doing something wrong in my marriage. I wasn't planning on being divorced at fifty-five after a twenty-one-year marriage, but it happened. The decisions that I made, or the ones I failed to make (failing to make a decision is still a decision) resulted in the most life-disruptive situation I had ever encountered.

I didn't Consider? the consequences of my actions. Where I am today is exactly where I DESERVE to be. I have to take responsibility for that. We all do. Each of us is at whatever point in life we find ourselves in as a result of the decisions we have made. And if you want to change where you are, you need to change some of the decisions you're making that are keeping you in that place. Many times, if we had taken the time to consider the consequences of those actions or decisions, chances are very good that we may have done things differently. This one question/answer session with ourselves can keep us from experiencing the pain of regret. Master it and you'll master the direction of your life FOR THE REST OF YOUR LIFE.

What might you start considering that could change your understanding of the consequences of your actions? How might that get you to the other side of a difficulty in your life? Consider? The consequences of your actions, and you'll start enjoying the life you deserve. Are you where you want to be in life, surrounded by whom you want to be? What decisions have left you there and what might you do differently in the future? Changes start now. Consider?

REFLECT AND RESPOND

1. Have you ever paused to consider the consequences of your next decision? If not, why?

2. What consequence would be drastic enough to change or create that intentional pause before you make a decision that could be life-changing?

_____

_____

_____

_____

_____

_____

_____

_____

_____

_____

_____

_____

_____

_____

_____

_____

_____

_____

PRINCIPLE 5
THE SECRET TO YOUR SUCCESS? GOOD DECISIONS AND DAILY DISCIPLINE

The secrets to success are starting and finishing. Good decisions help you start, and daily discipline helps you finish. **Daily discipline.** To change your life, you must change the things you do daily. If you don't practice discipline, and you don't do it every day, you will get out of the habit of having discipline. Getting the most out of every moment of every day is the foundation of the program. Good decisions and daily discipline, one is useless without the other. It does no good to have a great idea and make a good decision if you don't have the

> "The secrets to success are starting and finishing. Decisions help you start, and discipline helps you finish"

discipline to execute that great idea.

For instance, you can decide to start exercising, but if you don't have the daily discipline to do it, the idea is useless. It does virtually no good to exercise once or twice a month. You can have all the discipline in the world, but if you are being disciplined on bad decisions, it equally does you very little good. You must make good decisions and have the daily discipline to execute those decisions.

A good motto to remember when dealing with the people in your life, both personally and professionally, is, No vision, no decision. Vision is a fuel for us. People have to visualize themselves being successful. People believe what they see. When you get good at visualizing yourself executing choices and decisions, the results can be very powerful. There is no question that science has shown that visualization helps people be successful. We believe what we see in the flesh, and we believe what we see in our perfect mind's eye, when we see it often enough. That thought leads and helps you make the decision to execute that which you are visualizing. If you can see yourself doing it, then you probably can do it. If you can't see yourself doing it, then you are **RIGHT**, and you can't.

"No vision, no decision"

When leading your family, team, friends, or acquaintances, make sure you paint a very clear picture of what success looks like; no vision, no decision. And if you really want to make sure your team is successful, make sure your vision also takes into consideration the wants and needs of your teammates. It helps to be able to visualize having the things you want to be able to execute and get them.

This concept is also a very effective negotiating tool. When trying to make a point to people, make sure you are painting a clear visual image in their minds of what you're hoping to accomplish. If you're a real estate agent, telling your client, "Your black couch will fit perfectly in this long area of the living room" gives your client a personal mental snapshot of the living room with their furniture in it. In most all cases, help people see themselves doing something and you're halfway to accomplishing just that.

In all my trainings, one of the first major points I make is that success is predictable. In your job, your marriage, your friendships, and most any other situation in your life, we know what the face of success looks like. We've met it many times in our lives. Almost every job or task you will accomplish today has some type of road map that will lead you to success in accomplishing it. Countless people have walked before you in accomplishing the exact same thing. You may have even done so yourself previously. You just have to make the good decision to **start at right** and find what success is in that particular situation. Everything in your life works this way. The answer to what you are up against is at your fingertips. We are literally in an age where it is extremely easy to find information about what other people have experienced. You can research how to have success in almost every situation you will ever encounter. SUCCESS IS PREDICTABLE!

"Success is predictable"

The biggest reason people don't succeed in business and life is they don't expose themselves to existing information. Success is predictable. That's been clearly established (and you can't say it too many times, by the way). The answer is out there. Pick a topic, google it, and sit back and collect

ALL the information you need to make the **RIGHT** decision. You can literally become conversational on basically any topic in two hours of research and study. You just have to make the good decision and then have the discipline to execute that decision. The information is out there. Go get it. There is an instructional video on nearly everything somewhere on the internet. The biggest reason people don't succeed is that they don't take the time to do the work, do the research, and make an effort to find the answers.

For me, the secret of success is simple: Get up early every day and work your ass off. Nuff said. There's no real magic to success. It's a decision you make every morning. We've already discussed that success is predictable, and the necessary steps for success have been fairly well defined by the millions of people that have walked before you. All you have to do is take what you know has proven to be successful, then get up early and work your ass off every single day. That combination has proven to be successful throughout recorded history. Success is not determined by your title. You aren't only a success if you are a CEO. This equation and this book are completely aimed at achieving YOUR DEFINITION OF SUCCESS. Success is different for all of us. What I may hold as a measure of success in my life could mean absolutely nothing to you. And vice versa. You have to run your own race and be successful in the area and in the manner that is important to you, and in a manner that is achievable by you and for you.

In all my seminars and trainings, I start the event at the exact stated time, and I say to my audience, "The easiest thing you'll do all day is be on time." When I was creating this book, I was always on time for my book calls with Tiarra Tompkins, the very talented and capable VP of OnFire Books. She knew that I was always going to call her at the exact time she had arranged for the call, not a minute before, not a minute after. I would be sitting at my desk, watching the time to make sure I was punctual. Being on time is a discipline. And discipline, like **RIGHT**, is contagious. When you are disciplined in one area of your life, it is easier to expand that discipline into every other area of your life. You will be more confident as you master these disciplines. That is the start. That decision to always be on time tells people you are meeting with and all the people you are working with that you respect their time. Remember, respect is one of the most important things you can gift to someone else. Think about everything that you have to do in your day. Showing up on time really is one of the easiest, if not the easiest, thing you will do. It is one of the foundations of discipline in your life. It will serve you well for the rest of your life.

> **"Success isn't about what you do, it's about WHAT ELSE YOU DO"**

Success in life and business isn't just about what you do, it's about WHAT ELSE YOU DO. Since you know that success is predictable, you can't assume that you are the only one who has figured that out. You should know that you are not alone in knowing how to be successful. Lots of people, lots of companies, know exactly what to do to achieve success. Everyone in your business hears about the problem, so you be the one that suggests the solution. Don't talk about the problem...everyone's doing that. Dig and research and brainstorm, and be the one that offers a couple of different, potential solutions. What else sets you apart from everyone else who already knows? In fact, you must assume that everyone else is following your lead on the concept and studying past successes to map out future successes. So, all your competitors are doing the same things you are. You have to get out of the box and acknowledge that everyone is doing the same thing you are. You have to do something extra, the little things you do that make a difference. Success in life isn't about what you do, it's about what ELSE you do.

For example, when was the last time you got a handwritten thank you note? Some years ago, my then wife and I bought a Lexus for the first time. It was an extremely pleasant experience, but when it was over, I assumed it was over. Four days after we purchased the Lexus, we got a special delivery from a florist with a handwritten note attached. The plant was pretty, if simple, but the note was the difference maker. It was from the manager of the car lot, who had come by and spoken to us several times during the buying process. I remember thinking each time he came by how good he was at his job. He didn't try and assist the salesman in the sale. He didn't try and upsell us or entice us to add features to the car we had picked. He did something that actually had nothing and everything to do with our final decision. He was just nice! That's it. That's all the guy did. But it all made sense now. Everyone we encountered at the dealership acted the same way. Every single person there had an air of kindness about them. They all acted like they were actually looking for someone to be nice to. They all just did the **RIGHT** thing. As a businessman myself, I had great respect and admiration for the culture and attitude this dealership and all of its employees had toward their customers. It's almost like selling a car was secondary. You could tell they had all been trained to put making people feel welcome and appreciated ahead of most everything else.

As my wife set the plant on the bar and opened the note, I was struck by how excited she was to get this small gift. For the car we bought—her car—we should have gotten a tree or a small house or something. A little plant didn't seem like much. She took the note out of the envelope and carefully studied it. By her look, it surely had the cure for cancer amidst its secrets. She read it slowly, and broke into a big smile as she finished.

"What does it say?" I asked.

"Thank you," she replied.

"That's all?" I asked, a little surprised.

"Yes, but it's the way they say thank you," she elaborated.

"What do you mean?" I inquired.

"This note is just the culmination of their 'thank you effort.' They were saying thank you from the moment we walked in. They said thank you with their actions long before their mouth uttered a word," she continued.

The note said something to the effect of, "Welcome to the Parker Lexus Family. It was a true pleasure getting to know you and your family today. We look forward to many years of happy times and shared memories. Please don't hesitate to contact us if we can ever be of service to your family."

They didn't say anything about the car. Nothing. They knew better. At that point, it wasn't about the car. We had already bought it. They were genuinely interested in me and my family. It was an amazing buying experience from an amazing company and manager. It was a great example of the fact that **RIGHT** is contagious. The manager made sure that

> "People return to places that make them feel welcomed and appreciated."

he did everything **RIGHT** and his people followed suit. We bought three or four more cars from them over the next several years. People return to places that make them feel welcomed and appreciated.

How can you apply this to your own work? Let's say your company is bidding on a project. Everyone bidding on that project is as capable as your company and is relying on the same techniques you are. So, what's the difference? People buy differences. What else do you do that sets you and your company apart. What are the little things that people remember? One thing is they remember that you are the one that always *starts at right* in your decision making, yours is the company that ALWAYS does the **RIGHT** thing. Remember, when **RIGHT** gets in you, it becomes your identity. People begin to expect **RIGHT** from you and your company. The best indicator of future behavior is past, relevant behavior. So, people begin to factor this expectation into the decisions they make regarding you. BAMMMM, that's the difference…you get the bid.

In my career, I've always made it a point to do the what else for my clients from a place of **RIGHT**. It's not necessarily what you do in business that makes you successful; it's the what else you do that sets you apart and keeps your clients happy with your performance. Being SVP of National Accounts for my previous company, it was my job to service the accounts of our largest clients. Throughout the course of my twenty-one-year career there, that "what else" ranged far and wide on what I was willing to do (legally, of course) to help a client. My motto was, "Be the answer to all their problems."

> "Be the answer to all their problems."

One of my favorite and largest clients was a gentleman from the west coast who ran a very large, successful sales organization. Late one evening, Mark (not his real name) called me about his favorite family dog. I had been to his home a few times and knew the family really loved this dog. It was a black Lab, which was part of Mark's motivation for calling, because I had owned black Labs for over thirty years. He was calling to give me the sad news that their beloved dog had passed, and knowing that I was very involved with Labs, asked for some help in finding a new black Lab for the family.

His wife and two daughters were understandably very upset over the loss, and he wanted to find a replacement as soon as possible. "I'm on it, brother," were the first words out of my mouth, and I proceeded to literally launch a many-state search for a suitable replacement for their dog. Not only did I spend my very valuable time in this pursuit, I called my boss, the COO of the company, who was an avid Lab owner and breeder, and pulled him into the search as well. By the next day, word of the search had reached our CEO and he got involved in trying to find Mark a dog. You see, Mark wasn't just one of our largest clients. Mark was our close friend as well. We had all spent countless hours in meetings, dinners, trainings, and even vacations together with him and his family. We were genuinely committed to helping them find a dog as quickly as possible.

We were on a mission. Three senior executives spent many hours calling, researching, viewing websites, calling breeders, and whatever it took to help our friend and his family. This wasn't about business…this was about people. Granted, a dog was at the center of it all, but it was the people involved, our friends, that stoked our sense of urgency. Several days went by, countless dogs were considered then discarded, and we finally thought we had found the perfect Lab. We were thrilled with our efforts and the result. Then, Mark called and told us he and the family had found an out-of-state breeder they were comfortable with and they were on their way to get their new black Lab puppy. Counter to what you might think, our first reaction was pure relief that they had found a suitable dog as their new family member. We really didn't give it a second thought that we had each spent many hours searching in vain for a dog for them. This effort was one small example of the WHAT ELSE mentality we had toward our customers.

In life and in business, you should always be looking for the what else you can do to separate yourself from the pack. What will make your client, your friend, your teammate, or your spouse remember the extra effort you put forth to make their lives better? Focus on this, remembering that people buy/ remember differences. When you go the extra mile, when you focus on helping other people get what they want, your life will change in amazing ways. And besides, it's just the **RIGHT** thing to do. Helping people any way you can is the classic example of starting at **RIGHT**.

Other examples are the handwritten personal thank you notes that have become a lost art; offering to drive your friend to the airport (and pick them up) so they don't have to pay for parking; or mowing your sick friend's yard before they have to ask. It's the what else you do that makes you special. It's the what else that makes people remember how you made them feel. People may not remember what you say or do, but they will always remember how you MAKE THEM FEEL. The way we feel influences our decisions. Therefore, this same principle can apply to you and your decisions. What are the feelings

> "Most decisions are made based on moving toward pleasure or away from pain"

that are motivating the choices you make? Is it past experience? A good experience? A bad one?

In most cases, decisions are made based on moving toward pleasure or away from pain. Where did you eat lunch yesterday? Did you pull into a fast food drive-through because you were short on time or didn't want to spend a lot of money? Or, did you go to your favorite restaurant and get your favorite meal? One decision was made with moving away from pain as the motivator, and one decision was made with moving toward pleasure as the motivator. You have to learn how to study people and determine which of these two are their motivators. Pain is actually a greater motivator than pleasure because we will do more to avoid pain than we will to gain pleasure. This is only true, however, in the short term. That's what a lot of people—managers, parents, friends, and spouses—don't understand about pain. You can threaten people with the loss of their job or with having their phone taken away or with the idea that you will withhold your friendship from them. But, after a while, people get tired of fear-based motivation and will move to find other options. Long-lasting motivation comes from moving toward pleasure. It comes from inspiring people to want to do things with you and for you, instead of manipulating them with the threat of pain or loss.

Those are the two primary ways to motivate your people. You can inspire them or you can manipulate them. Picture this, if everyone on your team was told today that they had to turn in their reports or get fired, do you think they would be motivated to turn in that report? Of course they would! But this is very short-term success. If this type of motivation is used every time, eventually people will leave and find other jobs. Manipulation is pain. Love is inspiration. Inspiration and love can last forever. When I make someone else feel significant, and when I show them that they matter and that they have helped me achieve my goals, that will keep them inspired and motivated for the long term. To have a continuous, true team effort, you must inspire them through love instead of manipulating them through pain.

FOCUS ON RIGHT

RIGHT begins when you make that choice. People believe what they focus on. When you start focusing on RIGHT, then RIGHT starts to become a priority in your life, in your circle, and in your sphere of influence. But you have to start the process. RIGHT

> "People believe what they focus on"

doesn't just happen. The RIGHT fairy doesn't just show up and say, "Everything is just going to be RIGHT." Someone has to initiate the focus on RIGHT. RIGHT doesn't start until you do. It doesn't start until you start thinking about RIGHT, talking about RIGHT, and acting out on RIGHT. Take that first step. Go ahead. You know it's the RIGHT thing to do. This isn't magic. This program will change your life, but you still have to participate. You've got to put in some effort, then you'll see some amazing results. But once you start down the path of RIGHT, everything explodes. We know that RIGHT is contagious. If you will do RIGHT, and you make that your focus, then you will see **RIGHT** come back to you.

Aristotle is believed to have stated, "A work well begun is half ended." This concept, then, is possibly over 2,300 years old. Good decisions help you start, and daily discipline helps you finish. And starting at **RIGHT** is half the battle. Making the **RIGHT** decision and having the discipline to execute it is the key to finishing. Understanding what the task is, researching the best way to accomplish it (all good decisions), and then having the discipline to get started puts you on the path to success. Decisions are the starting point of everything we do. Discipline is the beginning of the end. Nothing happens without it.

The little things make the big things possible. Details are just discipline and details do matter. Having everything you need before the meeting starts makes all the difference in how the meeting will end. The little things give you the edge in a competitive scenario. When you make the decision to pay attention to the details, you are basically committing yourself to being successful in the big things. Most little things are somehow tied to one of the big things in your life. And virtually all little things teach you to be better at the big things.

Recently, I was encouraging my son to find a credit card company that caters to college students so that he can start building his credit. For a month, I kept asking him, "Do you have that credit card yet?" In our culture, credit matters. This is a very important detail in building his life. But he really didn't fully realize that because he had never had to deal with the consequences of not having good credit. Whenever he needed something, he knew I would take care of it. But now, as a smart young man about to start life on his own, it began to sink in to him that he had to take care of this (he knew I wasn't going to do it for him). He knew from many conversations and observing the lives of others that good credit was indeed a part of having a good life. So, he buckled down one day and got the card. He and I then sat down and designed a strategy to use the card appropriately, pay the balance off each month, and hopefully start building a lifetime of good personal credit. I'll never forget the day he called me many months later, and asked, "What was your credit score when you were twenty-three?" I wasted no time telling him to "do as I say, not as I do." My credit sucked at the ripe young age of twenty-three and I suffered the consequences for that. And as I started to remind him that he didn't have to suffer the same fate, he blurted out, giddy with pride, that HIS credit score was a solid 750 and climbing. That was definitely a proud moment for father and son! You have to have discipline to execute the details that matter. If you can execute the little details, then when something big comes along that does matter, you will be ready to handle it. Success breeds success. Preparation for the small situations make you ready and confident that you can handle the big ones.

"Focus on the goal, not the details"

At the same time, we can focus too much on the details instead of focusing on the goal. It's very important to me to be in good physical shape. I've worked out since my high school days and it's a big part of my life. If I spend too much time focusing on the details of my working out, it may drag me down, and I might dread the details versus the outcome. I want to focus on the outcome of the work on those details. I want to look at the result of my effort, not focus on the pain of the details. The details matter, but you can't let them ruin the outcome of the work. What do those details bring you? They bring you to your goal. The details were my son applying for and receiving his first credit card. The goal was to build a good personal credit score so he could enjoy the things in life that a good credit score allows. Mission accomplished on both fronts.

No pain, no change. If you really want to work on your discipline, make yourself do something every day that you hate doing. When my son, Grayson, was young I'd make him pull weeds in our landscaping as one of the chores to get his allowance each week. He hated pulling weeds. He would put it off all week, then make a mad dash on Friday or Saturday to pull them and get his allowance. So, with this principle in mind, I said he now had to pull weeds every day. He was focused on the task he hated, not focused on the money, which was his goal. Then I made the mistake of saying, "I don't care if you pull five weeds a day, you have to pull them every day." I shouldn't have been surprised when I came home and my son handed me five weeds. The devil was certainly in those details.

But discipline isn't always about pain. It's also about forming consistent habits and learning to use your time well. You probably have a good chunk of driving time in your day. Try turning that driving time into **RIGHT** time. When I worked at my old company, my commute was fifty-two minutes long, one way. Do you have twenty to thirty minutes (or longer) of idle time that can be transformed into **RIGHT** time? Make a decision that, as of today, drive time will now forever be time well spent. Traffic is no longer frustrating for me (change the way you talk to yourself). I used that fifty-two minutes as my devotion time. I could typically fit two messages during that time, and I walked into work every single day feeling great. Maybe you want to use that time for music or an audiobook.

It doesn't matter what you are doing with that time, as long as you are getting something good and **RIGHT** out of it. Otherwise you will hate that time and it will feel like wasted time.

Use that time to get your mind **RIGHT**, your life **RIGHT**, an argument **RIGHT**, and to lay out the **RIGHT** thoughts for the big meeting you have coming up. Don't waste any of that time in the car. You will never get that time back. Did you invest it or did you spend it? If you turn it into **RIGHT** time, learning time, and growing time, the investment of that time will never leave you. Traffic is now a welcomed extension of you honing your craft of **RIGHT** thinking. Feed this new mindset with whatever medium that is available to you and valued by you. Time is your most valuable asset, NEVER WASTE IT.

"No doesn't mean no. No means you didn't give me the RIGHT information, at the RIGHT time, to say yes"

If you stop right now, the last no was **RIGHT**. It is discipline that allows you to go forward beyond whatever perceived roadblock you may come across. You are going to hear no throughout your life, everyone does. It will happen in life and in business and more times than you will ever be able to count in every area of your life. You have to frame what that no really means. It doesn't mean no. For almost everything you want to do, there will be a time and place for you to do it. You have to learn how to frame that no in your head. No means, "You didn't give me the **RIGHT** information at the **RIGHT** time to say yes." Whether you're selling your opinion, your influence, your cars, or your house, no never means no. At least that's how you have to frame it in your head. If someone tells you no, and then you quit, that no was right. Failure is learning. Learning something from an experience is never a failure. Now, for the sake of the current times, everyone please know that no does mean no when it's in reference to what a man or a woman is consenting to. Respecting someone's boundaries is first and foremost the **RIGHT** thing to do.

This book you are holding in your hands is a perfect example of that. I have failed at writing a book on this material three times. I first wrote a parenting book with a co-author, completed the book, and for reasons I won't discuss, failed to even attempt to bring it to market. Two years of hard work went down the drain. Then I attempted to write a series of Sunday School lessons on the material, got halfway through it, and realized that wasn't the **RIGHT** market for the material. I failed again. Then I wrote a Christian book with my pastor, finished that book (it was pretty good), and decided to try to get into the medical marijuana industry. Out of respect for my pastor, I shelved it because I knew he wouldn't want to co-author a Christian book with someone who was in that industry. I had to respect his position on that. It was failure number three.

Did I consider those attempts failures? No. They were all lessons on how I needed to change the way I was doing things. Now I got it **RIGHT**. I have a children's book titled, *Just Do the Right Thing* that has been published...I FINALLY GOT IT **RIGHT**! You must have the discipline to keep asking, keep trying, and keep thinking of a different way to present your idea, proposal, or product in a manner that will entice someone to say yes. You may not have the **RIGHT** information at the **RIGHT** time. But you've got to ask the questions and keep trying. Sooner or later, the answer will be, Yes.

What good decisions can you start making today that will lead to and turn into the daily discipline of doing the **RIGHT** thing? What no have you taken at face value that you can transform into yes by instilling more discipline? Who is the one person in your life that has told you no that you can now re-approach with your idea or plan?

REFLECT AND RESPOND

1. What area of your life do you have the least amount of discipline in that you would like to change?

2. What good decisions can you start making today that will create the small victories that lead to the daily discipline of doing the **RIGHT** thing?

_____

_____

_____

_____

_____

_____

_____

_____

_____

_____

_____

_____

_____

_____

PRINCIPLE 6
SHOW ME? YOUR FRIENDS AND I'LL SHOW YOU YOUR FUTURE

Have you ever stopped to really consider your inner circle? Your inner circle are the people you choose to keep in your life. They are your most trusted confidants...can they be trusted?

You are BRANDED by the company you keep. This is critically important. Do you want to be successful? Then hang around successful people. Ask any teacher or leader and they will tell you, a big part of success is something that will be reflected by those you surround yourself with. You learn from the people you spend time with. If you want to pick up skills that you need to work on, like sales, you need to find someone who is great at those skills. Then you need to invest some time in them and create a real friendship. Watch them, listen to them, copy them,

"You are BRANDED by the company you keep"

and ingratiate yourself to them. The important people in your life are writing a very important chapter in your story. Make sure it's worth reading.

The Bible says, "He who walks with wise men will be wise. But the companion of fools will be destroyed." How many people do you know who have suffered this fate? How many good kids have been corrupted by bad company? It's one of the most common things you hear from parents of troubled youths and teens. "They were a really good kid until they started hanging around with _____!" How does this same phenomenon affect us adults? Think about the client you get and become friends with. Can you really be influenced by your friends to call in sick to work, cheat on an expense report, or go to a club that your wife wouldn't approve of? Sadly, the answer is yes. Our friends, the people we hold dearest besides our family, and sometimes, more so than our family, are truly a huge influence on our lives. As a small example, have you ever found yourself using a catchphrase or motto that a friend repeats often? We tend to assimilate the behaviors of those around us.

"He who walks with wise men will be wise. But the companion of fools will be destroyed"

We are very associated with who we associate with. You can't be friends with shady people and not think that others that see the association will make the assumption that the qualities and bad habits they possess must also be yours. It is just a natural progression.

It has been said that when you conquer that which you fear most, the death of fear is certain. One big reason we haven't moved away from this group of friends is fear. People typically don't like change, which is why they tend to keep the same friends. As humans, we have a deep-seated need for inclusion. We want to be part of something greater than ourselves. We want to belong. Our friends give us this comfort, this sense of being able to count on someone. Losing that comfort seems unthinkable. As a result, changing this group of friends in hopes of finding another group that is better suited for our future sounds pretty stupid. Why move away from the people who already accept us for what we already are? At least, that is what we tell ourselves. What are the fears that keep us stagnated? Fear of being alone. Fear of not being accepted. Fear of change. Think about the change that happens in a divorce. You could have had dozens of friends who are couples, but once you become single, it changes. You're no longer included in certain activities because you don't have some of the key elements in common with the rest of the group. Life changes, good or bad, can change your circle of friends. In the end, though, your life is your own to live.

> "When the sun sets on your life, the only thing people will remember you for is the influence you had on them and others"

When the sun sets on your life, the only thing people will remember you for is the influence you had on them and others. The direct meaning of influence is "the capacity to have an effect on the character, development, or behavior of someone or something." That is an awe-inspiring thing, and a powerful thing. Your legacy will be partly defined by the influence you had on other people. They won't remember what you did on a particular day, or what you wore to a certain occasion, or what you said in a given moment. What they will remember is what you have taught them. Through your actions and your words, please remember that every moment of every day is potentially a chance to influence someone, to possibly change their life forever. That's what you'll be remembered for—your influence.

I was talking about business with my son, Grayson, one day, and out of the clear blue sky he says, "Dad if you're the smartest guy in the room, you're probably in the wrong place." Wow, what a profound statement from a college kid. And how true…If you want to continue to grow, you need to surround yourself with people who are smarter than you in one area or another. There is usually someone in the room or at the table who has the need to be the smartest person there. We have all had bosses and leaders like that. We also have had leaders and bosses that hire based on finding someone who is smarter than them in the area that they are weak in. Their strength should complement your weakness. The opposite should be true as well. This is how I hire. If someone has strengths that I don't have, I want them on my team. Their weaknesses aren't as important (they can always be coached up) because I am not playing to those. I am playing to their strengths. If you have a leader that has a problem with your intelligence or the connection you have with people or needs to be the smartest person in the room, it's going to be difficult for you to grow in that situation.

You want to be successful? Then hang around successful people. It's pretty simple. That's the first thing you can do to increase your odds of achieving your goals and dreams. Success breeds success, and success becomes a habit just like

RIGHT becomes a habit and just like discipline becomes a habit. We are creatures of habit. Successful people get in the habit of doing things better, different, and longer, whatever it takes. If you want to improve your life, you have to do things like that!

Look around…are you really the smartest person in the room? If so, who is going to teach you new things? Who is going to have the courage to correct you when you are wrong? Who is going to

> "If you want to be successful…hang around successful people"

push you to be the best possible you you can be? Do yourself a favor: Surround yourself with people who are smarter than you, who have achieved a higher degree of success than you have. Find people who have character traits, work habits, and skill sets that you hope to someday have as well. These are the people who have blazed a trail before you, a trail that you hope to follow.

I know you're asking yourself, "And where do I find these people?" It's called networking. It's called acquaintances from church. It's called joining the Chamber of Commerce. It's called getting off your ass and meeting people. People are in your life for a reason, a season, or a lifetime.

"When someone is in your life for a REASON, it is usually to meet a need you have expressed. They have come to assist you through a difficulty… To provide you with guidance and support… To aid you physically, emotionally, or spiritually… They may seem like they are a Godsend, and they are. They are there for the reason you need them to be. Then without any wrongdoing on your part, or at an inconvenient time, this person will say or do something to bring the relationship to an end. Sometimes they die... Sometimes they walk away... Sometimes they act up and force you to take a stand.... What we must realize is that our need has been met, our desire fulfilled... Their work is done. The prayer you sent up has now been answered and now it is time to move on.

Some people come into your life for a SEASON because your turn has come to share, grow, or learn. They bring you an experience of peace or make you laugh. They may teach you something you have never done. They usually give you an unbelievable amount of joy. Believe it, it is real. But only for a season.

LIFETIME relationships teach you lifetime lessons, things you must build upon to have a solid emotional foundation. Your job is to accept the lesson, love the person, and put what you have learned to use in all other relationships and areas of your life.

It is said that love is blind, but friendship is clairvoyant.
Thank you for being a part of my life... Whether you were a
reason, a season, or a lifetime."
~ UNKNOWN AUTHOR

If someone is in your life for a reason, it is to solve a particular issue. God put them in your life to give you insight into solving a problem, achieving a dream, starting a company, or some other important happening in your life. They are typically instrumental in that endeavor and then tend to fade to the background, not disappearing completely, but not occupying a seat among your closest friends and associates. If they are in your life for a season, it's to help you with a major life issue: divorce, job change, family tragedy, or betrayal on a large scale...something that will take you time to cope with. A lifetime association is the support system you count on throughout your life: parents, siblings, closest friends, and other very close relatives and associates. These are the people that you rely on throughout your life. These are your mentors, your spiritual advisors, the best man or maid of honor in your wedding, and the people who know and love the real you. They have the benefit of knowing you through a life cycle. They've seen you grow and change and they've probably been instrumental in those changes. These are the people you call at 3:00 in the morning when your car breaks down and they don't hesitate to respond.

Friends can change and transition from a seasonal to a lifetime friend. It just depends on the way the relationship grows and changes. Things in life change. If you can't change with it, there will be a consequence. As a leader, you have to be able to identify the change master in your group. Things always change in business. For that matter, things always change in life as well. Change your people or change your people (meaning you either teach your people to change with the times and conditions, or you have to change out those people and get new ones).

> "You must take change by the hand, and if you don't, it will assuredly take you by the throat"

Change happens. And if your people can't adapt to change, then you have to change your people. You have to go find some people who will embrace new ideas, new products, and new challenges, people that will embrace new. In business, things change. In life, things change. In relationships, things change. And for you, for me, and for the rest of our teams, it's change or die. Wow, pretty sobering isn't it? But it's the truth. The axiom in business is "Change or die." Literally. If you don't embrace change, your business will die. Winston Churchill said, "You must take change by the hand, and if you don't, it will assuredly take you by the throat."

Show me your friends or teammates and I'll show you your future. You have to know how to change the people in your life and your business when things change. If the people you have can't adapt to this new world, you will have to make the sometimes tough choices to find people who can make those changes with you and not push against those changes and forward progress.

You only have to have one change master on your team to smooth these change transitions. One person can be the spark that gets the rest of the team on board. You must embrace change, encourage change, expect change, and celebrate change. Then reward those early adopters that help you sow the seeds of change throughout your organization. It only takes one. Show me that one talented change master, and I'll show you a group of teammates lined up behind them to change your company. To change your family. To change your circle of friends. To change any group of people. It only takes one strong person and the rest will follow.

"That's what this book is all about, changing the way you talk to yourself."

If you're going to be that change master, then in many cases, you have to change the way you talk to yourself. The first place we lose the fight is in our mind...in our way of thinking. That's what this book is all about, changing the way you talk to yourself. To change your actions, you have to change the way you think. To change the way you think, you have to change the way you talk to yourself. In a lot of cases though, you won't be the change master. It will be someone on your team. And that's what you want. That's why you surround yourself with smart people. You have to find and be aware of who that change master is because they will help your team adjust and adapt to the changes. Allowing a teammate to lead the charge will embolden them, build their self-confidence, and make them a stronger leader themselves. It also gives hope to the rest of the team that anyone and everyone can have the same opportunity. Everyone may have to change the way they talk to themselves. This is exactly what you want.

HOE TO THE END OF THE ROW

As long as I live, I'll never forget Larry Odom. I worked on Larry's farm during the summers of my junior and senior years in high school. To this day, it was the hardest, dirtiest, hottest, and most Godforsaken work I've ever done in my life. The first summer, we cleared his farm fields of tree stumps and rocks and rats and snakes and every other horrible, man-eating thing you can think of. The most scared I've ever been was one day that summer. We had just pushed over a very large tree stump with the bulldozer. Larry told me to knock the dirt off the roots and tie the chain around them to drag the stump off. As I approached the stump, I heard the now familiar shotgun blast, and felt the percussion just a couple of feet away. I turned to see the largest copperhead snake on the planet, now missing its head. This was the twentieth-plus time Larry had shot something during this effort.

About that time, I felt a sharp pain in my right leg, and could tell something besides my leg was inside my pants. Seconds removed from an encounter with a huge snake, I immediately thought I had been bitten by one as it crawled up my pants leg. As I frantically tried to get my pants off, I could hear Larry laughing hysterically while offering no help at all. I was able to grab the attacker from the outside of my pants, squeeze it, and keep it from eating the rest of my leg. Shucking my pants quickly, I found a rat the size of a small bus squirming to escape my clutch. Larry's laughter caught my attention again, and looking up, I heard him say, "You got to hoe to the end of the row, boy." Not having any idea, nor caring, what that meant, I finished my first and last hand-to-hand combat match with Ratzilla and went off to examine my wounds.

The next summer, working for Larry again was my best option for summer employment. This year though, he informed me that I would be solely working in a fifty-acre watermelon patch. My first thought was, "Fifty acres isn't a patch; it's a small country!" Larry informed me of the other conditions of my employment: He would pick me up for work, and he would bring me home every evening. Well, in my little brain, I was thinking that was like a small raise. I didn't have to drive my car or buy gas. So, I agreed. It was the biggest mistake of my young life. Now I was trapped. You see, Larry Odom was the hardest-working human on the planet. He picked me up and brought me home so I couldn't escape. I couldn't say I wasn't feeling well and leave work. I was trapped in the hardest, hottest, and loneliest job in the world, working fifty acres of watermelons. Do you have any idea how many rows of watermelons that is? Let me help you here. It's row after row after row after row after row…you get the point, right? And my job was from seed to sale. So, I got paid $2.00 an hour (it was 1976), and 10 percent of the gross profits at the end of the summer. So, my work began.

I planted and watered the seeds to get them growing quickly. It seemed like overnight and watermelon plants were everywhere. At first, I thought it was cool-looking. That lasted for about nine minutes. Then, before my very eyes, it was like there was an explosion of runners. Runners are the vines that grow from the plant that the watermelons actually grow on. There are many runners on each plant, and they can grow up to ten feet long. About this time, I was thinking, "How hard can this be? Mother nature does all the work." Wrong, town boy. You do all the work! It was about this time that Larry gave me my first real tutorial on growing watermelons.

"OK boy," he said (it was the only thing he ever called me), "you've got to walk every row, move the runners, hoe any weeds that have grown in them, then move the runners back so they have room to grow." I thought, "What the hell? Does he realize how many runners there are? Does he realize how long these rows are? How big this field is? Sweet mother, does he realize I have a date Thursday night?" My mind was swimming. I didn't sign up for this…at least I didn't realize this is what I was signing up for. But that was it…that was my job for three and a half months. And the worst was yet to come; the watermelons started growing.

Now, I had to move a runner with a two-pound, then ten-pound, and then twenty-pound watermelon attached to it. It was brutal. Well, about halfway through the summer, I got the bright idea that I'd fudge a little and not work all the way to the end of the row. Who would know? Who would care? There were enough watermelons to feed a third world country. Big deal if a few of them had some weeds in their stupid runners. That was a big mistake, HUGE MISTAKE, because I didn't stop to think that Larry would know. He knew everything. He could plainly see the weeds growing at the ends of each row. And unbeknownst to me, he knew that the weeds were robbing those watermelons of water and nutrients…duhhhhh, that's why I was hoeing weeds, so those watermelons didn't grow so large. BUSTED!

Finally, he approached me one day in a fatherly manner…I'll never forget it. He said, "Boy, you haven't been finishing each row." I started to challenge his claim, but his raised hand quickly silenced me. "I can tell, so don't argue with me," he said. "And what you don't realize," he continued, "is you're not cheating me.

"You've got to hoe to the end of the row"

You're cheating yourself. The last 10 percent of each row is your money, boy. That's YOUR bonus for all this hard work. And look how much smaller those melons are than the ones in the middle. You've got to HOE TO THE END OF THE ROW, BOY! Don't cheat yourself. It's the last 10 percent that makes the difference between a good crop and a great crop… between a good bonus and a great bonus. Don't ever forget this boy, you've got to HOE TO THE END OF THE ROW," he said again for effect.

AND I HAVEN'T FORGOTTEN. Forty-two years later, I still remember his leathery face, his fatherly words, and his sage advice, and that it was all meant to help me. You see, those words weren't about watermelons. They were about life. I didn't realize it then, but they applied to everything I have done or ever will do for my whole life. To be a good person, you've got to hoe to the end of the row. You can't stop 10 percent short and cheat on your taxes or betray a friend or cut corners in your job. To be a good leader, you've got to hoe to the end of the row. You can't expect your people to **start at right**, and you not do the same thing. To be a good spouse, you've got to hoe to the end of the row. You've got to consider their needs before your own, sometimes. You've got to find common ground on issues you once thought non-negotiable. You've got to give that last 10 percent to make sure you've done everything possible to solidify that union. To be truly successful in life, you've got to finish strong, finish that last 10 percent, and HOE TO THE END OF THE ROW.

How have your friends and the people in your life influenced you? Will they help you go the full distance to doing the **RIGHT** thing in your life? Or will you come up short? If you're coming up short, what changes might you make in the people you allow to influence your life? Are you inadvertently cheating yourself by not giving a task your all? A relationship? Are you doing **RIGHT** in all you can?

REFLECT AND RESPOND

1. What are the major influences in your life that hold you back or propel you forward? Explain.

2. If you have people or things holding you back, how can you work to remove those things and make sure that the **RIGHT** influences are empowering your life?

PRINCIPLE 7
LIFE IS? PERFORMANCE BASED

Life is performance based. It just is. If you don't accept that, you are doomed to the consequences it will bring… and believe me, there will be consequences. Just do the **RIGHT** thing isn't just a moral standard. It's a performance standard as well. We hate to admit it sometimes, but it's the reality of the world we live in. If you don't perform at work, you're going to get fired. If you don't perform in your marriage, you're going to get a divorce. If you don't perform as a friend, your friends will find other friends. That's just the way life is.

There is a standard of performance that we are all held to, and it's called **RIGHT**. Just like **RIGHT** maps out the starting point of your moral or personal decisions, it also sets the standard for your performance metrics as well. But one very important point to acknowledge is that performance is measured on a personal ability level. People are only as skilled as their personal talents allow them to be.

"Work at it with all your heart"

Some students will never get straight As. Their best performance is going to be a B, or maybe even a C. And that's fine. The question is, did they do their best? Did they do **RIGHT** by themselves in their effort? This principle encourages you to work at it with all your heart. Do the very best you can, each and every time, and usually, that will suffice. If everyone on your team will **start at right**, and do the best job they possibly can, you can imagine what the results of the team's efforts will be. Millions of people before us have set the performance standard for most things. The **RIGHT** way to perform is, in most cases, clearly defined and that information is available to us. We just have to be willing to look for it. You must work at it with all of your heart. That is all you are expected to do. If you are giving it your best effort, you will perform to the level to get the acceptable outcome that you want.

What do the steps of success look like? I know there are probably many different variations of the answer to this question, but one thing that has proven very effective for a notable group of people is: Visualize, verbalize, realize. What I think about (visualize) is what I speak about (verbalize), and through those actions, I will bring about what those things are (realize). Tiger Woods, one of the greatest golfers of all time, credits visualization as one of his greatest assets in repeatedly making great golf shots. As he stands over his next shot, he has a very specific routine that he goes through which includes seeing the ball take the path he wants it to. Life is like a golf shot…once you see it in your perfect mind's eye, you are more likely to be able to do it. You can train your mind to see yourself doing

> "Where your mind goes, your ass will follow."

things you haven't done before. And, as we all know, where your mind goes, your ass will follow. And remember, your thoughts have to be stronger than your emotions. This exercise helps hone that skill. By continually seeing yourself be successful in many different areas of your life, you're training your mind to engage in that process as a way to direct your life with decisions, instead of conditions. So how do we get there? As Zig Ziglar said, "You've got to be before you can do, and do before you can have." It's got to be in you before it can come out of you. You've got to feel it. Be still, and listen to that still small voice inside you. It's in your heart, not on it. Whatever it is you're trying to accomplish must become part of your identity. When **RIGHT** is in you, it becomes part of your identity. That which you can BE will also be possible to DO. You can DO because you learned that skill set, you took that course, or you read that book. That's part of what puts the BE in you. You have to learn that skill set before you can utilize it and capitalize on the benefits. And once you have it, once it's part of you, then you can DO And then, you get what you've wanted all along: You can HAVE. You can HAVE whatever it is that is the result of your do. But you can't have until you do, and you can't do until it's in you, until you can be. Most of the learning I have done as a father I have done through what I learned from my father. My father put that BE into me, and because of it, I could be a good father to my children, the do. And because I was able to be and do, I now HAVE a great relationship with my own children.

From what well do you draw the water to nourish what you mean to cultivate? Life or business is a school. What did you learn today? And how did you learn it? Did you observe a teammate skillfully diffuse a tense situation with a large client?

Did you get words of wisdom about a marital situation from a trusted friend? Or did you reference a recently read book to get information for a presentation? Point being, you learned something today. You learn something every day if you'll be still and observe. Be still and

> **"Life is a school. What did you learn today?"**

listen. Be still and take advantage of the information that is available to you. Be still and you'll be very successful doing all these things. Make that the rule, not the exception.

I'm sure you've heard the phrase, "Excuses are the tools of the weak and incompetent. Used to build monuments of nothingness. Those who excel in it seldom excel in anything else but excuses." Well, "MEET ME IN THE MIRROR," and let's talk about that. Don't tell me what you can't do; show me what you can do. There are only two people you can't lie to: God and the man in the mirror. Far too often, that voice in your head tells you "you can't do it." Whatever the situation may be, and for whatever reason, we tend to pay attention to that voice because many times, that voice is the easiest voice to listen to. It's the easy way out. Many times, it's going to be very hard to do the thing we may be trying to do. And the only thing keeping us from trying is knowledge and the man in the mirror.

"Meet me in the mirror" and ask these questions: Why? Why not? Why not me? Why not now? WHY can't I be the CEO of my own company? WHY NOT invest in that extra degree or level of training to be qualified for that position? Why can't that person be me? I know our business, I work well with our customers, and my teammates respond to me, WHY NOT ME? And there's no better time than now. WHY NOT NOW? The question has to be asked. What is the why behind these questions? You have to ask these. Why not start right now?

What opportunities are you squandering for yourself by feeding into that small negative voice, or by giving it dominion over your life and its possibilities? What power can you harvest for yourself by quieting that voice and making a choice to feed your future prospects? MEET ME IN THE MIRROR!!! Invest your time; don't spend it. What did you invest in today? Did you write a few pages of that novel you've had in your heart for fifteen years? Did you take that hour for yourself and go to the gym? Did you sit quietly, alone, still, for thirty minutes and pray or meditate? Did you do this, or some other small thing that will bring you a measure of peace, or somehow make you better? In short, did you invest in the most important person in your life…YOU? It's a fine line to invest in you or be caught up in you.

This idea goes beyond the idea of self and permeates all of your relationships, even in business. People don't do what you tell them to do. They do what you pay them to do. For the most part, that is. In a leadership role, especially in business, nothing is truer. This is your job, and this is what I pay you to do. Make sure it gets done. And many times, what you pay people to do is all they're going to do. Granted, you can inspire people in many situations and they will do what you ask. And those who report to you will always do what you tell them to do. That's not the point here. The point is the extra, the big picture. You can motivate people to perform one of two ways: manipulate them with incentives or inspire them by appealing to their *sense of right*. And by that, I mean what's **RIGHT** and good for THEM, not you or the company.

The people in your company who report to you do what

you say because you're the boss. You manipulate them with authority, fear (threat of losing their job), perks, and pay. But they do the things you ask because they have to…not necessarily because they want to. Conversely, if you choose to inspire your people, they do things because it's in their heart, it's in their best interest (if you're a good boss, you've made sure of that), they love it, they love you, and they love the company they work for. It's in them, not on their to do list. Never forget that when something is on you, it turns into a behavior. But when something is in you, it becomes part of your identity. It's a character trait, it's who you are. That's how you want your team, be it family, friends, or co-workers, to feel about that which you're leading them in.

"Get to, got to; understand the difference" Do you have an attitude of Get to or Got to? Attitude is key to the approach to any task you take on yourself or any task that a teammate is tackling on your behalf. It's the difference between Get to and Got to. You Get To get better, work harder, see your dreams come true, and meet all of your expectations. Do you get to do something or have you got to do it? Understand the difference. Performance is tied to how we talk to ourselves. Got to affects the mental capacity about the way you approach any given task or situation. Get to, got to is all about mindset. When you Get to, it's in you. It's in your heart. It's something you love, and you get to do it. When you've got to do something, it's because you have to.

I'm sure at work you have been assigned a task that you'd rather not do. You can choose to think about this in one of two ways. First, have you got to do it, meaning it's dreaded and only being done because you need a paycheck? Or do you get to do it, utilizing your skills, being a valuable member of the team, and putting forth a genuine effort because **RIGHT** is in you and you want to get the job done well?

It's our attitudes that define our approach to the more trying things we need to accomplish on our individual paths toward success. Can you work through those difficult tasks or will you fail because you quit? The only place success comes before work is in the dictionary. Life is performance based. And success is predictable. If you work hard at whatever job it is (work at it with all your heart) you have, if you do the things your management has clearly laid out for you, and if you start with what you know to be **RIGHT**, that's all that will ever be asked of you. Success follows hard work. Success follows commitment. Success follows doing the **RIGHT** thing ALL THE TIME, even when it isn't easy or popular. And that's the primary caveat for lifetime performance and success, willingness to do the **RIGHT** thing all the time.

RIGHT is present in every moment. All we have to do is get out of the way. In every situation, **RIGHT** is waiting to come onto the stage. **RIGHT** is waiting for someone to release it. Recognizing this, and what **RIGHT** actually is in that particular situation, is the setting for true performance and success. The freedom to do the **RIGHT** thing lies within you. And the vast rewards of **RIGHT** come along with that freedom.

REFLECT AND RESPOND

1. How will you use the *Power of right* to enhance your performance in everything you do?

2. What principles that you have learned so far will be instrumental in helping you perform better?

PRINCIPLE 8
THE THREE MOST IMPORTANT THINGS IN LIFE ARE? FAITH, FAMILY, AND HONOR

What are the most important things in your life? How do you decide what facets of your life take priority? What ideals do you hold above all others?

Faith, Family, and Honor top my list. This is the most important principle in this whole book, other than the guiding principle itself "Just? Do the **RIGHT** thing." In my opinion, these three things really are the most important things in life, and they all magnify the essence of **RIGHT**. When I teach on this principle in seminars or trainings, I often get more questions and opinions than on the rest of the principles combined. If you asked one hundred people what the three most important things in life are, you will almost assuredly get fifty plus different answers, and a lot of them may not match up with these three.

I think that throughout this program you have seen *the power of right* at work. All of the other principles are very commonly accepted life principles. People see them validated by many other respected sources in their life. They're taught respect, responsibility, consequences, discipline, and all the other principles at home, or by other respected adults in church, on a sports team, the list goes on and on.

Once we get to this question though, it always raises more questions. When did I understand the power of this question?

This question/answer was actually the very first question I started with my daughter, Tori. She was six years old and the light of my life. Her mother and I had divorced a couple of years earlier, and even though I had very generous visitation rights, it wasn't like being there with my daughter every day. I already called her at least once a day, but it's tough to get a six-year-old to say more than yes or no in a conversation. Out of the blue one day I asked her, "Baby, what are the three most important things in life?" When I said this, I wasn't even thinking about the answer. It was like God shared this seed with me. Using my sales background and knowing the power of a question, I thought asking her deeper questions would deepen our conversations. Well, you can guess that the response I got from an unsuspecting six-year-old was vastly different than her, trying to go deeper, dad's expectations.

Tori, very calmly, looked at me and gleefully replied, "Uhhhhh, deer hunting, ummmm duck hunting, and bedroom dodgeball." She was so proud when she finished that list. We always had fun together, and those were three of the things that we liked doing the most. What else would you expect from a six-year-old who listed the three things she enjoyed doing most with her dad. "No, baby," I answered. "The three most important things in life are God, family, and honor."

Thus began a twenty-five-year journey of communicating with my children through the power of a question, repetition, and planting the seeds of **RIGHT** thinking. For the purpose of this book and the material I share with the secular world, I have substituted God with Faith in this program. Faith is nothing more than belief, an unquestioned belief and trust in the foundation of those beliefs. It is belief beyond reason. No matter what proof we have, we still have to have a measure of blind faith to believe in the unseen. Faith is that sincere belief. And we all get to choose what we have faith in. People of faith, like myself, choose to place that faith in God. Others choose to have faith in other forms of religion or other ideologies, or debunk religion completely. But everyone believes in something, and I teach that one of your strongest beliefs should be a belief in yourself. You have to believe in and have faith in yourself first.

This principle is about life priorities. If you're really going to discuss the three most important things in life, you'll be plumbing the depths of your beliefs. Studies have proven that what you believe is the strongest thing in your life. For the purpose of this book and this program, the answer is faith, family, and honor, and let me explain why:

FAITH

Beyond belief, our biology supports just how important beliefs are to the neurological working of our minds. One study conducted by Jordan Grafman, PhD, director of the cognitive neuroscience section of the National Institute of Neurological Disorders and Stroke stated when subjects heard phrases like "God will guide my acts" and "God protects one's life," there was a decided lighting up of the God spot in their MRIs, which was similar to those seen by happiness. This revelation corroborates that a deep-seated belief in something perceived as good really does have positive health benefits for people.

Faith involves intellectual assent to a set of facts and complete trust in those facts. Faith is basically nothing more than a complete belief in something. And the great thing is, you get to choose what you believe in, what you have faith in. Some people (myself included) associate faith with religion. In that case, faith is the act of believing when it is beyond reason to believe. We have no concrete proof, nor will we ever, that Jesus actually walked this earth, turned water into wine, made blind eyes see, or healed the crippled so they could walk. No one can point to proof of that outside the scriptures of the Bible. But hundreds of millions of people have faith in the teachings of the Bible. I believe with all my heart that the teachings of the Bible, The Word, are true. I have faith.

> "Faith is believing when it may be beyond reason to believe"

One very important type of faith that is integral to success is a complete belief in yourself and the important things in your life. A big part of your success is having the unshakeable faith that you CAN be successful, and that you can complete the task, do the job, and win the game. It has been said that "whether you believe that you can or cannot accomplish something, you are correct." This is the first belief that you must master. No one else will believe in you if you don't believe in you. This is literally the foundation of self-esteem, self-worth, and self-love. What you truly believe is what is real for you.

You must also have faith in the foundations that support your life: your family, your job, and your friends. You have to believe that your family will always be there for you. You have to believe that the people running the company you work for know what they're doing and can keep the doors open and you employed. You have to believe that your friends won't betray you, and that they've got your back. It's this fundamental faith in the people, entities, or institutions involved in your life that enables you to have peace of mind, knowing that you're not in this alone.

What you believe has more power than what you dream or wish or hope for…you become what you believe. What you truly believe in the bottom of your heart is the guiding force in your life. This is why faith is one of the three most important things in life. It is the beginning of you becoming the person you are destined to be. It is the foundation that you will build the rest of your life on. It is the starting point of all that you wish to do in this life.

> "What you believe has more power than what you dream or wish or hope for…you become what you believe"

One of the things that greatly affects our faith is fear. Fear can almost be described as a lack of faith. It is the antithesis of faith and is also one of the greatest challenges in life. This is what holds most of us back from accomplishing our goals and pursuing our dreams. And failure is just one of many fears. There is also a fear of success. If we succeed, then success will be expected of us going forward. Even in success, fear robs you of your goals and holds you back from doing what you dream. Fear is primarily caused by ignorance and pre-conditioned ideas, often stemming from childhood or early life experiences. The more you know, the less you fear. The emotion of fear is far worse than the reality of that which you fear. And fear is one of the greatest enemies of success known to man.

The more you know, the less you fear. Knowledge truly is power. Fear is what keeps us from writing that book, from asking that girl out, or from applying for the management position. Fear of the unknown, fear of failure, fear of success, and fear that we won't measure up to expectations might be the most debilitating emotion we have.

> **"Fear is the antithesis of faith, and is one of the greatest enemies of success known to man"**

Your first goal is to make others believe that you believe with all your heart. Can you tell the difference? Can you really tell when someone is telling you something, showing you a new idea, or presenting some options to you, and you don't believe that they believe what they're posing? They lack conviction. They lack that sense of unquestionable truth. It's called doubt. Conversely, you can also tell when someone believes with all their heart what they are saying or doing. Unabated enthusiasm is what you display when you believe with all our heart. When you believe, you can convince others to believe. That is how you close the sale, convince others. You have to believe in what you are selling or you won't convince anyone else.

Your true belief is going to change the way others see what you believe in. Faith starts with you. You have to believe in yourself to pursue success.

FAMILY

The second component of this principle, Family, is about your support system. This isn't always necessarily going to be your biological family. Unfortunately, everyone isn't lucky enough to have a great biological family as their support network. I am extremely blessed in this area. The need for humans to belong to a unit structure, a family if you will, is extensively documented. We NEED people in our lives, people that we can count on for emotional support, financial help, and protection from any outside source seeking to harm or challenge us. We need a family. We need someone to lean on, someone that's always got our back. But what exactly is a family? One definition describes family as "a group of people, usually of the same bloodline (but do not have to be) who genuinely love, trust, care about and care for each other." This can be a family of friends, a church family, a school family, extended family members (aunts, uncles, and cousins), or a sports team family.

"The human need to fit into a family structure and be accepted encourages us to conform to the beliefs and behaviors our society has established as our code of RIGHT"

Family helps hold you up. Any organized group can serve as the support system we all need to feel protected, included, and significant. This phenomenon of belonging to a family of some type is extremely important to all humans.

We can't do this life thing alone. No matter what we think, we just can't. That unconditional support is needed, and it is actually this need to fit in and be accepted that encourages us to conform to the beliefs and behaviors our society has established as our code of **RIGHT**. The bond that links your true family is not one of blood, but one of respect and happiness and trust in each other. True family transcends bloodlines. The fundamental human need to belong to some type of family is the reason this is one of the three most important things in life. True family is the connection to something greater than yourself. And each part of the family is equally important, whether the leader/patriarch or matriarch figures, or the smaller support roles. Everyone has a place; everyone has a role. The one constant is you're not in this alone, whatever this is. No judging, no stereotypes, and no excuses, just LOVE, just unconditional LOVE. This is a fundamental need of all people. Without that support, society as a whole starts to break down. Because of the fundamental human need to have some type of family structure, family is one of the three most important things in life.

HONOR

In Shakespeare's *Julius Caesar*, Caesar proclaims, "I love the name of honor more than I fear death." Honor is honesty, fairness, and integrity in one's beliefs and actions. In other words, just doing the **RIGHT** thing. Living a life of honor is nothing more than always, in every situation, doing the **RIGHT** thing. Honor is what you get when **RIGHT** is truly in you, when **RIGHT** is your identity. A person with **RIGHT** in them wouldn't dream of doing the wrong thing. They wouldn't dream of disrespecting people and will truly treat those around them with kindness and dignity. Honor means

> "Honor is all things right"

always doing **RIGHT** by those around you and speaking **RIGHT** into those around you. Honor is all things **RIGHT**.

Honor is one of the highest compliments one person can pay to another person. It is recognized in all cultures, all circles, and all walks of life as the highest regard one person can show another person. Honor is inextricably locked with **RIGHT**. To treat people with honor is to always have their best interest at heart, to always do **RIGHT** by them. For these reasons, it is this author's opinion that Honor really is one of the "three most important things in life."

REFLECT AND RESPOND

1. What have been the three most important things in your life?

2. How are those things connected to faith, family, and honor?

_____

_____

_____

_____

_____

_____

_____

_____

_____

_____

_____

PRINCIPLE 9
KNOW? YOUR PURPOSE IN LIFE

Most people believe they have a purpose in this life. The trick is recognizing what that purpose is. As is within, so is without. The happiest people on the planet are the ones that have mastered the fine art of aligning their outer actions with their inner values. Life gets easier, work becomes crystal clear, and relationships are smoother when your actions mirror your beliefs. Then, you can be who God truly meant for you to be. Your purpose in life will follow your deepest beliefs. It is the core of who you are, and that is all tied to your beliefs. When you reach this point, you don't have to think...you just do. You just are. What you're doing comes so naturally, so easily, that it's almost effortless. It's MEANT TO BE. It's LOVE! When you are able to turn WHAT YOU LOVE

"When you are able to turn what you love into what you do, you have truly found your purpose in life"

into WHAT YOU DO, you have truly found your purpose in life. When I am speaking to a group of people, I get out of my own way and it just comes. I just connect. I can feel my audience getting in tune with me and my message. I truly believe that my God-given talent and purpose is to speak to people. That is the gift He gave me. When you are doing what you are purposed to do, the rest of your life tends to fall in place.

Understanding that, always remember that anyone who is hungry to learn is easy to teach. The best student is the hungry student. If you feel that you haven't found your purpose in life, stay hungry and keep learning. Keep experiencing new things that may lead you to new passions. The best groups I have ever spoken to are the ones who are hungry. It's been my experience that young professionals who are the most hungry tend to be people that have studied something. They have gone to college, vo-tech school, trade school, or through some type of educational process. You can see the hunger that was birthed by their education. Their studies taught them how to do things in the business world, and now they are anxious to find the places to do these things. They have read the books and articles. They believe the people that have walked before them. They believe that success can be theirs and they act accordingly. They dress for success. They become a student of their craft. They surround themselves with smart, like-minded, and hungry people. Good leaders are adept at wrapping their goals and ambitions around the wants and needs of the people helping to reach those goals. Helping people do things that they are hungry for can actually help people find their purpose. Sometimes people are searching, looking for that thing that gives them satisfaction for their life's effort. Remember life is always about learning and growing. Teaching them new things can expand their horizons and possibly open doors they didn't know existed. You can help someone discover their purpose by matching their skill set with a need that you have or the company has. When you wrap your mission statement and goals around what your people love, then you will see them work hard and work at it with all their heart.

If you don't have a reason to keep your heart beating, it won't. People say, "Follow your heart." I like to say in my seminars that your purpose will follow your heart. It will be something that you love. What we have to be careful and mindful of—and of course as parents, teachers, and mentors—is that we align reality with our skill set and with what we think our purpose is, and it may not line up with what we are doing. We have to make sure that it lines up to that which you are truly meant to do, is ordained by the creator, and is your true destiny. It will be something that has been laid on your heart and has now gotten into your heart. It has become part of your identity. It's deeper and stronger than a want. It's a calling. It's something that you're truly passionate about.

It is important, however, to keep a healthy dose of reality handy when you're considering your purpose. If you don't have an athletic bone in your body, it is highly unlikely that your purpose in life is to be the middle linebacker for the Dallas Cowboys. You may have always dreamed of being a football player, but that is not your purpose in life. If it were, God would have equipped you with the rest of the tools to make that dream a reality, to bring your purpose to life. Singing and I are a great example of this. If I could snap my fingers and have any God-given talent, I would want to sing. I think it is the most sincere and beautiful form of communication on the planet. But that's not the communication talent God gave me. He wanted me talking without the music. Your purpose is that thing that gets you out of bed every day. It could be your family, your close friends, your boat, or your golf game. It's that thing that drives you beyond yourself.

"Purpose often intersects with talent."

Purpose often intersects with talent, but there is a difference between talent and skill. Talent is a God-given gift. You are born with it. When I was younger, I wanted to be a basketball player. I was tall and fast, but that didn't mean I had the proper skill set for it. You have to have a voice of reason for what you think your purpose is. Skill is taking the talent you are given and working very hard to make it better. You can learn a new skill set. I can learn to put in a kitchen sink by reading about it. That doesn't mean I should quit my job and become a plumber. I am tall and fast, and was actually pretty good at basketball, but it wasn't my purpose in life to become a professional basketball player.

You can't learn talent. You either have it or you don't. This is a very important part of truly finding and understanding what your true purpose in life is. It's about being honest with yourself and truly understanding and knowing that person in the mirror (perfect meet me in the mirror moment here). We have all had the dreams of becoming a professional football player, a world-famous neurosurgeon, or an internationally acclaimed actor. These dreams are driven by things we only think we are passionate about, things we only think we have the skill to pursue. Your dream of becoming a professional football player died with the realization that you didn't have the skill to be one. You showed some talent in football as a youngster, but you weren't able to refine that to the point that it became a true skill that allowed you to compete at the highest level. Add that to the fact that you're 5'8" and 173 pounds, and you can probably feel pretty safe in accepting the fact that God's purpose for your life is not being a Dallas Cowboy. Understanding this will help you prevent the pitfall of choosing a path that isn't meant for you.

An unknown author wrote, "The purpose of life is not to be happy. It is to be useful, to be honorable, to be compassionate, to have it make some difference that you have lived and lived well." I personally think this is saying if you will concentrate on these things: honor, compassion, usefulness, and living well, they will bring you the happiness you seek in your life. RIGHT is contagious. And when you put RIGHT out into the world, it creates happiness for others and returns happiness back to those who send it out. Happiness isn't something that just happens, it's created. Living your life in a manner that is purposeful and beneficial to others is the seed of contentment and thus contributes to the happiness in your own life.

> "Living your life in a manner that is purposeful and beneficial to others is the seed of contentment and thus contributes to the happiness in your own life."

In his book, *P.S. I Love You*, H. Jackson Brown recalls this advice, given to him by his mother: "Twenty years from now, you will be more disappointed by the things you didn't do than by the ones you did. So, throw off the bowlines. Sail away from the safe harbor. Catch the trade winds in your sails. Explore. Dream. Discover."

Don't be the person who failed to throw off the bowlines. I was almost that person. For twelve years, I put off developing *The Power of Right* because I was busy, because I had a good job and a family to support, because I didn't have a sense of urgency, and because I wasn't sure of what to do with it. I basically used whatever excuse I could find to justify my inaction. But deep down, it haunted me. And if I had continued down that path, I would have reached the end of my life and been devastated that I didn't share the crown jewel right in front of me. To speak to and share *The Power of Right* with other people is one of the main purposes in my life. I know that. God put this idea in my heart over twenty years ago, and he didn't put it there for me just to enjoy it with my kids. I really believe that universal ideas and concepts like this are meant to be shared with everyone. And

"When you find your true purpose in life, your reality becomes better than your dreams"

shame on me or anyone else who doesn't do that. It's a mistake for anyone to let the seeds of their talent go unplanted.

When you find your true purpose in life, your reality becomes better than your dreams. It's out there for all of us. We just have to find it, wait for it, dig for it, beg for it, and do whatever we have to do to get it. Your purpose is effortless, even when it's not. When you're doing something you love to do, even when it's hard, you do it. As the saying goes, "Love what you do and never work a day in your life." You don't think about it, you just do it. Our true purpose in life is our "it." It's that thing that gets you out of bed every day. It's that place in your mind that you go to when life is a storm.

One of the most profound moments in my career happened over ten years ago in Raleigh, NC. I remember it like it was yesterday. It was one of those weeks from hell where I had to travel to three cities in one week. That's the worst thing for a business traveler. I left early on a Monday to go to North Carolina and was set to return from Salt Lake City on Friday. So many cities, so many meetings, so many people, and so much to do. I love my work, but this was four straight weeks of heavy travel (many of you reading this right now can relate), and it was taking a toll on me. I very seldom do three cities in one week. I do two stops six to eight times a year, but mostly I keep it to one destination per week. This stretch had me knocking on the door of burnout, and that's a dangerous destination for someone in my business.

LARRY WALKER

I was in Raleigh-Durham International Airport when I first heard Larry Walker, one of the airport's restroom attendants. I say heard because you could hear him all the way from the terminal as he greeted and said farewell to his customers. Yes, he treated everyone that entered that restroom like you and I would treat a customer. "Good morning, sir" was his greeting, and "God bless you, sir" was his choice of sending you on your way. For some reason, when I saw Larry, a wave of peace came over me. It was early, I was tired, my mind was blank, and I had to pee…just saying. It lifted my spirits to see someone—anyone—who was so genuinely happy at this early hour. Larry was happy to see everyone that entered his restroom, his office, and his kingdom, if you will. I noticed immediately that it was spotless, and it didn't smell like a typical public restroom. This man took great pride in his job. He was so proud and so humble about this place, this destination that was so important to so many other people every day. That day, Larry Walker changed my life. He was living in his purpose. It reminded me that I could live in mine as well. Your purpose is **RIGHT**. And **RIGHT** is contagious, and when you put **RIGHT** out into the world, it comes back to you.

As I walked in, Larry greeted me in his high-pitched, welcoming voice. As our eyes met, I nodded at him and smiled. "Good morning, sir" is all I could muster. I was still soaking in this rather unusual experience. In that instance, however, I knew this would somehow be a memorable moment in my life. He warmly replied the same way, "Good morning, sir." I eased by him and walked into an open stall. With my mind wandering, awash with relief, and at peace with myself and my surroundings, I finished my business and turned to see this amazing man that God put into my path.

I noticed that the room was empty, except for the two of us. I couldn't help but notice that he was looking me squarely in the eyes, piercing, inviting, and connecting. From nowhere, Larry said, "Sir, you know Jesus is alive?" A little startled, I replied, "I know he is. He lives in my heart every day." To which Larry shot back, "No, he's alive in this room RIGHT NOW!" WOW! Talk about a wake-up call. Talk about something touching your heart. Talk about God putting a random human in your life to remind you that He is ever-present. I stood there, somewhat dumbfounded. I

"A prince of a man, who just happened to be an airport bathroom attendant, taught me about purpose"

didn't really know how to answer. I also knew that at any second, it would be over. One of Larry's customers would enter and end my one-on-one date with destiny. Then I realized, no words were necessary.

Larry had delivered the message he was ordained to deliver. He had touched the heart of the person he was supposed to touch. He had reinforced what I already knew to be true, but needed to be reassured of that morning. Then, it came. Larry broke off from our stare and went about touching someone else's life. "Good morning, sir" rang his now familiar greeting. My moment with Larry Walker was over. But my time with Larry has lived on in my heart, in my soul, and now on these pages. A prince of a man, who just happened to be an airport restroom attendant, had touched me in a way that I'll never forget. A man that had truly found his purpose in life now helped me remember that it doesn't really matter what our purpose is. What matters is that we find it and share it. Thank you, Larry, and may you and yours be blessed beyond measure, just as you have blessed me.

I left that restroom feeling like I was walking on air. It's hard to describe how I felt. I couldn't believe how that exchange had re-energized me. I felt like I should write a country song or something: "I Found Jesus in an Airport Bathroom." Gone was the dread of the upcoming week. Gone were the feelings of exhaustion and burnout. One man, one innocent but profound conversation, and one moment that I was smart enough to capture, changed my perception of purpose for the

> "Everyone can have a chance to touch someone's life, and to make someone's day."

rest of my life. The lesson is that it doesn't matter what your job is. From the CEO of a major corporation, to a mother raising two kids, or to an airport restroom attendant, everyone can have a chance to touch someone's life, and to make someone's day.

Be still. We have to open ourselves to these moments. If you will just be still, you won't miss them. Listen to the inner voice. You have to change the way you talk to yourself. You have to be still so you can hear the voice in your head and the voice in your heart, so you can meet God, or your representation of God, wherever he might be—even in an airport restroom.

What is your purpose in life? How can you know it, find it, and pursue it every day? Are you chasing a false purpose? Is your purpose aligned with what you know to be **RIGHT** in your life?

THE SHADOW

The following is a prayer/meditation that my son wrote on the last of a five-day, intense, and advanced yoga training conducted by internationally acclaimed instructor Seane Corn. It's special because my son wrote it (of course), but more so, because when I read it, I instantly realized he wrote it for me. And he wrote it for himself...and his sister...and his nanna...and YOU! Some things in life are universal, and the shadow is one of them. The "shadow" is real...and we all have one. Please enjoy.

"Few things in life are universal and the shadow is one of them"

"What are you avoiding? What are the things that loom in your background that you allow to create fear, anxiety, and

depression within you? What is your source of resistance...
YOUR SHADOW? The spirit guides not only by light, but
by darkness as well...manifesting itself as tension to get your
attention. The time for avoidance and momentary relief has
passed. It's time to channel your Warrior Spirit and confront
the darkness, your shadow...steadfast...patient...with acceptance and faith that the current is pulling you toward your
awakening. Breathe...Love the Shadow...respect it...accept
it...then, LET IT GO!!! It will set you free." - Grayson Faught

I read these words with great pride in the young man my
son has become. I believe that part of my purpose in life is
to be a good father. That part of my life is one of my highest
priorities. At the ripe young age of twenty-three, Grayson is
wise beyond his years. He has an innate sense of **RIGHT** about
him that comes from his experiences, his observations, and
the teachings of several good men in his life. From an early
age, he was blessed with having great relationships with
strong, **RIGHT**-minded, God-fearing, and honorable men:
Haley Shaw, Steve Kirk, Papa Flu, Pastor Craig, and my own
father, to name but a few. I have great respect and appreciation for the time and love these men have invested into my
son's life. I see their stamp on many parts of his personality.
I hear their words of wisdom coming from his mouth. You
see, my son is part of their purpose in life as well. I truly
believe that. God has laid it on their hearts to take my son
into their circle of influence. Grayson loves these men, lis-
tens to these men, and respects these men. And it is their
purpose and his great fortune that their paths have crossed,
as they all drive down life's highway.

So, what casts your shadow? Are you to the point in your
journey that you can talk about it? Can you write it on these

pages? Ouch, 'bout to get real here, folks. I know, it's tough…I struggle with mine constantly. I pray about it every day…often, many times a day. You have to understand that the shadow doesn't go away until you shine light on it, and until you break down the barriers of fear and unforgiveness and acknowledge it.

"You have to understand that the shadow doesn't go away until you shine light on it"

It's right there behind you…everywhere you go…in everything you do…you can never escape it. You can only conquer it…or it continues to conquer…CONQUER YOU. But when you finally do get the best of it, then it becomes part of your shield. It becomes that part of your life that protects the sacred places in your heart. Your shadow then becomes your protector. It will still never leave you, but now it adds a new and different dimension to your life. It is the voice now of completion, of confidence, and of all that is **RIGHT** and good in your life. For if you can bring light to this fold of your life, you can do anything. You can forgive anyone. You can overcome any obstacle, any setback, and achieve any goal. Nothing is as big as your shadow. NOTHING! Your shadow is part of your purpose in life…you have to know that. It is there for a reason: to teach you, to humble you, to awaken you, and to move you forward or backward, whatever your need may be. Embrace it…learn from it…be still…you are now complete.

REFLECT AND RESPOND

1. What is your shadow?

2. How will conquering your shadow help you find your purpose in life?

PRINCIPLE 10
MAKE TODAY? THE BEST DAY OF YOUR LIFE

Have you ever had a moment that changed the course of your life? A 6:00 a.m. flight out of Boston, with a one-hour drive from Worcester, was one of mine. Those times meant that I had to be up at 2:30 to leave the hotel at 3:30, turn in the rental car at 4:30, and go through security around 4:50. I don't do early flights very well (I've got a little diva in me). As I approached the security podium, I noticed this slightly built, middle aged woman warmly greeting each passenger as they came up to her. When it was my turn, I stepped up to the podium, and while handing her my driver's license and boarding pass, I gave her a half-hearted, half-awake, "Good morning, ma'am. How are you today?" I'll never forget what Felecia (she had a name badge) said to me, and more importantly, how she said it. She actually leaned forward a little, looked me squarely in the eyes, smiled as big as her face would allow, and said "Sir, it's the best day of my life."

My first thought was she had to be lying and I even asked

her if she knew it was 4:50 in the morning. Then, taken aback by the obvious sincerity of her statement, I asked her why it was the best day of her life. Without hesitating, she said, "Every morning, sir, when my feet hit the ground, I say, 'I am blessed that I woke up this morning, I am blessed that me and my family are healthy, and I am blessed to have this job. Sir, I make sure that every day is the best day of my life.'" I was so impressed by the sparkle in her eye and the conviction in her voice. She really believed that she could make every day the best day of her life. I said, "Wow! That is so cool, Felecia. I do motivational seminars and I'm going to tell your story everywhere I go. I'm going to point out to people that having the best day of your life is a choice and we all get to make it every day."

And I have done just that. I've been telling Felecia's story for well over fifteen years, and now hundreds of thousands of people have heard it. Try this for one day. Every time someone asks, "How are you doing?" you have to reply, "It's the best day of my life." But listen folks, the delivery has something to do with it. You can't say it like your dog just died. You've got to put some energy into it. It's got to sound like it really is the best day of your life. I was pulling through a McDonald's several months ago and the young lady at the drive-through asked how I was doing. With my usual zeal, I said, "Ma'am, it's the best day of my life." She said, "Awwww. Sir, it's just an egg McMuffin." For the record, it was the best egg McMuffin I'd ever eaten in my life.

Can you really "Make today the best day of your life?" This principle is the anchor of this program by design. Everyone and everything needs a destination. "Where are you going with this information" is a question I'm sure many of you asked as you began reading this material. When you started this program, you expected something out of it. You expected it to take you somewhere you haven't been before, somewhere exciting, somewhere beneficial to your life, and somewhere that lives up to the giant expectations of **RIGHT**. You expected it to add something to your life that might be missing. If it's **RIGHT** it has to be good for you, doesn't it? Well, the best day of your life is the ultimate destination. It's that place in your mind and heart that is the culmination of all you know to be true and **RIGHT**. And if you do it **RIGHT**, you can get up tomorrow and do it all over again.

Part of the impact of Felecia's story is to plant the seed in everyone who reads this to know that your words matter. A wonderful, unassuming lady interacted with me for less than two minutes over fifteen years ago, and the words she spoke changed my life forever. I've actually trademarked the phrase, "Make today the best day of your life" because of Felecia and the impact she made on me with that statement. The school of life is in session every day. What will you learn today? Whose life will you change with a kind, influential word? Whose destiny will you impact by sharing a life tip—your life tip—that tip from a story like Felicia's that only you have? Remember, only you can do you!

"Whose life will you change with a kind, influential word?"

This principle also highlights the fact that every single day we have a choice. Being happy is a decision. Making today the best day of your life means making the conscious decision to be happy and making the conscious choice that none of the things that happen today are going to change that decision to be happy. Whatever condition that may arise today will not overtake your decision to be happy. This is the classic example of your decisions dictating your destiny instead of your conditions. Once we drown out the bad voice in our head (change the way you talk to yourself), we can focus on the good one. The anchor of the program is making this day the best day of your life. And the start of it is just doing the **RIGHT** thing. If you will get **RIGHT**-focused and **RIGHT**-centered, if you will learn to **start at right**, and use that one-word trigger, Just, it will make everything else fall into place. We all make a choice every day about whether or not we're going to let our circumstances, our job, our spouse, our kids, or anyone else taint our attitude or outlook on life. We make a choice, a decision, to be happy or not. And the premise of this book and program is that if you will "Just Do the **RIGHT** Thing" and then follow the other eight principles as well, you really can MAKE TODAY THE BEST DAY OF YOUR LIFE. Living your life by these principles will give you the greatest chance at a happy, successful life, as you define success.

The attitude of gratitude is one big factor in helping make every day the best day of your life. Having an attitude of gratitude is a very important daily exercise. By being grateful for all the things in your life, you are less likely to think about any problems or setbacks you may be experiencing. And even if you do think of them, those thoughts aren't as likely to derail your attitude when you balance them with a healthy dose of gratitude. Try starting your day with this simple prayer or mantra. That's what I do. Before I even get out of bed, I pray, "Thank you Lord for all my blessings. Thank you for my health and the health of my friends and family. Thank you for all the opportunities you have put in my path. Thank you for this glorious day that you have blessed me with." I start my day by being grateful for what I do have and not giving energy to the things I don't have.

KEEP YOUR EYES ON THE PRIZE

I have come to know and believe wholeheartedly that true happiness is a "be." It's a decision: "I'm going to BE happy." Your conditions have nothing to do with that decision. One thing that will help you become more decision-centered in your life is learning to focus on the outcome, not the details. Too often, we think of things and situations in terms of what it takes to accomplish them. Doing that puts you in a condition-minded situation. Details are conditions. The outcome, the goal, is a decision. You made a decision to go to college, get a degree, and pursue a career in a field you love. Then the process starts: figuring out how to pay for it, going to class, studying long hours, the emotional roller coaster of taking tests, and sweating out the results. You know the routine. You have to endure these details, these conditions, FOR YEARS before you reach your goal of graduating with a degree.

"Stay focused on the prize"

If you solely focused on these details, it would be easy to lose heart, get discouraged, and quit college. Tens of thousands of people do this every single year. They lose sight of the goal, the outcome, by getting blinded by the details. The grind, the pain, the discomfort, and the "I can't take this anymore" feeling from the details blur the vision of the goal. In life and in business, you have to keep your eyes on the prize. You have to remember why you started down this path, and what you loved about the goal that made you start the process. In most cases, why we started doesn't change. We still want to graduate with a degree. We still want to expand our company and reach the elite status in our industry. What changes is our fortitude, our willingness to sacrifice, and our stomach for discomfort and risk. People believe what they focus on. STAY FOCUSED ON THE PRIZE, and the details become nothing more than that, details.

Another good habit to develop involving your focus is to not look in the rear view mirror. Happy people tend to think about what they want and how they're going to get it. For the most part, those things are ahead of you, driving down life's highway. I want to continue to be a good father

> "Happy people think about what they want and how they're going to get it"

and a good friend. I want to enjoy continued success in my career. I want to meet the woman of my dreams and get married again. I want to write a New York Times best selling book on leadership called *The Power of Right*. I want to do a TEDx Talk (which I did)! All of these things that I want are ahead of me, in my future, driving down life's highway.

If I focus my thoughts on these things that I want, then think about what it takes to accomplish these things, my mind is going to stay pretty occupied. In essence, this is the way I've chosen to talk to myself about things that move me forward in life. Remember, the quality of your life is dictated by the voice in your head. What you think about, you will speak about. What you speak about, you will bring about. Think about the things you want in life.

Conversely, unhappy people, for the most part, tend to

"Unhappy people think about their problems and their pain" think about, and thus focus on, their problems and their pain. People believe what they focus on. Almost all of your problems are associated with things that have already happened in your life. Some examples are your divorce, your bankruptcy, the betrayal of a friend, your indebtedness, the fight you had with your girlfriend, your poor grades in school, your late car payment…pick something else if you'd like. Most of these things originated, and are still, behind you, in the rear view mirror. If you were to drive down life's highway, like a real highway, looking only in the rear view mirror, you would almost certainly crash and not reach your destination. Continuing to think about these problems doesn't change any of the circumstances that caused them to happen. *The Power of Right,* with its link to mindfulness, gives you the easiest route, on a repeated basis, to escape the chains of your past by bringing you into the moment. It is helping you focus on the positive things in your life. STAY in the moment. Change the way you talk to yourself.

Every day, we all travel down life's highway. Several times throughout the day, we come to a T in the road and we have to make a decision on which way we will go. *The Power of Right* gives you a starting point that gives you the best chance to make the **RIGHT** decision, to take the **RIGHT** turn. One of the ten principles will be applicable for ANY situation that will ever come up in your life. Learning to live by these principles will literally give you a roadmap to success as you define it, for the rest of your life. This is how you make every day the best day of your life. When you know you have a reliable formula for happiness, you know you have a way to pull yourself back from the abyss called life. You have a way to level set the expectations of **RIGHT**.

SAVOR THE MOMENT

When life gets you down, when you have a three-city week ahead of you, and when everything that can go wrong has gone wrong, we have to learn to savor the moment. You see, we all have those moments in life where everything was **RIGHT** and good, where happiness, security, comfort, and _____ (you fill in the blank) were the guiding forces in our lives. We have to be able to savor those moments and revisit them when the inevitable trials of life begin to creep into our lives and minds. These moments remind us that life is good, that we are blessed, that things will ALWAYS get better, and that through our decisions, we're in control. Everyone reading these words, please write down your three or four most fond moments in your life, moments that when recalled, instantly bring a smile to your face and cheer your heart. Have those moments ready when life happens. Use them to change the channel in your head, to change the way you talk to yourself.

One of my favorite moments involved my son, Grayson, when he was a young boy. He was five or six years old and one of his favorite things to do was go deer hunting at our deer camp. My brothers and I had a place in the Ozark Mountains, and some of my greatest family memories are steeped in the lore of deer camp. For thousands of families in Arkansas, deer camp is a sacred tradition. It's where boys and girls, friend or family, and young and old gather to bond over good food, mythical stories, and hopes and dreams of harvesting that lifetime buck. On this particular morning, we were up early, getting all of our hunting gear ready and finishing up some breakfast. Grayson knew how important it was to be in our stand before daylight, and he was very excited as we finished loading everything on the four-wheeler and began to mount up. "I'm driving, Dad," he blurted out, like that was something I didn't already know. That's another Arkansas tradition; we teach our kids to drive motorized vehicles at a very early age. The pure joy on that child's face was priceless to me. Some of my fondest moments with Grayson and Tori involve hunting and riding four-wheelers. As we eased out of camp and down the mountain to our favorite stand, it struck me how older Grayson seemed than his years. He instinctively scanned his surroundings as we entered a turn in the trail. He knew to look for other four-wheelers driven by one of his uncles or cousins. These were all things we had practiced and talked about dozens of times. It was a proud moment for this father. As we got closer to our stand, he knew exactly where to park so we wouldn't spook any deer that might be in the area. He turned off the four-wheeler, quietly dismounted, and began gathering his gear. He knew exactly what he was responsible for, and he knew that we had entered the quiet zone; no talking above a whisper, no coughing or sneezing, and no stepping on branches or leaves…the greatest attention to every little detail. We stealthily walked down the trail toward our stand, the only light coming from a distant sunrise millions of years in the making. This was my favorite part of deer hunting; early morning, settled into our stand, quiet, alert, anticipating, and waiting for the sun to peek over the mountains. Hunting with my kids is definitely a top five "love to do" thing in my life. It was one of the cornerstones of **RIGHT** teaching for my kids when they were growing up. It teaches discipline, respect for Mother Nature and other hunters, patience, and a heightened sense of awareness. It teaches kids to respect an animal's life and the time-honored tradition of taking it.

We sat motionless for a couple of minutes and I could feel Grayson looking up at me. I looked down and he whispered, "Dad, this is so cool." I replied, "What son, hunting with your dad?" To which he quickly corrected, "No, it's so cool that Mom lets you play with guns." Out of the mouths of babes. I couldn't contain myself and let out a laugh as I reached down and hugged him as he giggled too. Then he slowly pushed me back a little bit, looked up at my face through eyes of wonder, and reached up and gently patted my cheek with his cold little hand. He said, "Dad, you are my best buddy." Nothing else mattered at that moment in time. My life was complete. Everything I had learned, everything I had taught my kids, and everything that was **RIGHT** and good in my life was just validated by the innocent words of my six-year-old son.

We didn't see any deer that day, but that was a moment I will savor forever. There came a moment while you were reading this book when you realized that **starting at RIGHT** is a great way to live your life. But more importantly, there came a moment while you were reading this book that you realized that you too can be great. Savor that moment, and it really can be THE BEST DAY OF YOUR LIFE!!!

REFLECT AND RESPOND

1. How do you feel about your day when you first get up in the morning?

2. Do you need to change that first moment from a negative to a positive?

3. In your life, how will doing the **RIGHT** thing contribute to making today the best day of your life?

_____

_____

_____

_____

_____

_____

_____

_____

_____

_____

_____

_____

_____

_____

_____

_____

_____

_____

_____

_____

_____

ABOUT THE AUTHOR

Brian Faught is a father, author, TEDx speaker, corporate trainer and speaker, and successful businessman. His purpose in life for the last 20 years has been to spread the message of **RIGHT**. Through seminars, training Fortune 500 companies or one on one coaching sessions, Brian has taught tens of thousands of people how to *start at right* in all their decision making. His engaging, humorous speaking style is loved by all and opens people's eyes to the vast rewards of living a **RIGHT** centered life. Please contact Brian at **justdotherightthing.org** for your keynote speaker needs, sales or customer service trainings, or personal mental tune up. It's a changing day when you decide to put **RIGHT** to work in your life and company.